UNBINDING
your
HEART

The Unbinding the Gospel Series
by Martha Grace Reese, JD, MDiv

In more than 15,000 congregations, 50 states, 49 denominations, 8 countries...

"Evangelism" is anything you do to help someone move closer to a relationship with God, or into Christian community

MOTIVATION – *then* INVITATION

Enrich Spiritual Lives & Deepen Spiritual Relationships → Invite!

Evangelism books presume everyone *wants* to do evangelism, so they tell you *how* to do it. Nine years of national, Lilly Endowment-funded research in ten denominations have demonstrated conclusively that most people would rather get a root canal than think about evangelism! You can tell people to "go be missional" until the cows come home. You can give them great suggestions, brilliant lists of activities to invite friends into faith. How's that working for us?

Let's get real: none of us are going to do anything until we *want* to. Your church won't do statistically successful evangelism until a large percentage of people (1) pray, and (2) talk comfortably about their faith experiences, and (3) think about people beyond church walls. We need to know *why* to share our faith. Prayer & deepening spiritual relationships in small groups stir motivation. It's "*pre*-evangelism." Motivation moves us to action. Once we can answer "**WHY** share my faith?" we'll start wanting to know "**HOW** can God use me?" Now you're ready for evangelism—listening, sharing your faith and actual invitation. The *Unbinding the Gospel Series* helps your whole congregation address first the **Why** (motivation) *then* the **How** (faith sharing and invitation).

Start with *Unbinding the Gospel,* progress to an all-church saturation study with *Unbinding Your Heart.* This creates motivation—people will *want* to invite! *Unbinding Your Soul* will help with your small group stream of invitation and discipleship.

WHY Churches: A Year of Motivation (*"pre*-evangelism")

STEP ONE– *Church Leaders' Studies:*
Unbinding the GOSPEL (red ribbon). Start with a test study with 8-10 "quick adopter" leaders. Pastor leads. (DON'T preach or write newsletter articles – you'll create resistance! Remember: "Evangelism" = "Root Canal".) Pastor: read the introduction and chapters 1 & 4 of *Unbinding Your Church* now.

- Study *GOSPEL* in eight weekly sessions
- Do the exercises at the ends of the chapters
- Pray with 40-day prayer journal

Lead more small group studies of *GOSPEL* with your church leaders and teachers (20% of your worship attendance).

See www.GraceNet.info for *Best Practices* - step by step instructions to use the Unbinding Series

STEP TWO—*All-Church Saturation Study:*
Unbinding Your Heart (purple ribbon) is a six-week version of ***Unbinding the Gospel*** with a new individual prayer journal. We see significant changes in churches that bring the "unbinding" experience to at least 85% of worship attendance. Each week, for 40 days, people will:

- ■ Pray each day's scripture and prayer exercise & work with a prayer partner
- ■ Study a chapter with their small group
- ■ Worship — sermon, music & prayers centered on the week's chapter

red ribbon

SUPPORT FOR STEPS ONE & TWO— *Pastor's and Leaders' Guide:*
Unbinding Your Church (green ribbon) offers research-based best practices for small group leaders, prayer teams, youth leaders, pastors. It provides comprehensive organizational aids, coordinated resources for children, youth & families, worship, full music plans in four styles & 7 sample sermons.

HOW Churches: A Year of Invitation
(Relational Faith Sharing)

Unbinding Your Soul: Your Experiment in Prayer & Community (yellow ribbon) is for:

- ■ Churches that have finished their all-church saturation study of ***HEART***
- ■ New churches
- ■ New members' classes
- ■ Young adult / college groups

purple ribbon

SOUL is the small group foundation for your year of invitation! Seekers would love to try a no-obligation experience of substantial spiritual discussion, prayer and community. ***Unbinding Your Soul*** prepares church members to invite their friends into a four-week small group experience with short study chapters, an individual prayer journal, prayer partner activities & group exercises. A second four-week small group process is included for groups that want to keep going. NEW! Sermons, liturgies & updated facilitators' guide available at www.GraceNet.info.

green ribbon

See www.GraceNet.info
for videos, sermons, children's materials,
free resources and info on a new
Lilly Endowment study

yellow ribbon

"Not even the grumps can kill it!"
"We never want to go back to normal."
"We're baptizing adults and we have an influx of young couples visiting."
"I haven't been so energized about ministry in 15 years!"

For
Russ, Elizabeth and Sarah

UNBINDING *your* HEART

40 Days of
Prayer & Faith Sharing

Martha Grace Reese

CHALICE
PRESS
ST. LOUIS, MISSOURI

Cover photograph: GettyImages
Photograph of author: David Bjerk
Cover and interior design: Elizabeth Wright

www.chalicepress.com

15   14   13   12   11   10   13   14   15   16   17

Library of Congress Cataloging–in–Publication Data

Reese, Martha Grace.
  Unbinding your heart : 40 days of prayer & faith sharing / Martha Grace Reese.
    p. cm.
  ISBN 978-0-8272-3805-3
  1. Evangelistic work. 2. Church group work. I. Title.
  BV3790.R358 2008
  269–dc22

                                                                2007038681

Printed in the United States of America

For Best Results
download free "Best Practices" memo
at www.GraceNet.info
Before You Start

Contents

Acknowledgments

How do you thank all the people involved in a book based on 1200 interviews? This book arises from a national four-year study, the Mainline Evangelism Project. Over 1200 people took time to talk and write about their faith, their ideas and feelings about God, the church and evangelism. Thank you to each of you. You welcomed us into your offices, homes, churches and inner thoughts. I hope this book reflects the best of what you told us. I pray that it will be helpful to you and to others who love God and want to help others move into deeper relationship with God and the church.

The heads of five mainline denominations have been supportive of the project since the very beginning. They read descriptions of the Mainline Evangelism Project, listened to ideas, responded generously with advice, access and support. Thank you, Wes Granberg-Michaelson (RCA), Dick Hamm (DOC), Cliff Kirkpatrick (PCUSA), Roy Medley (ABCUSA), John Thomas (UCC) and Sharon Watkins (DOC). Stan Noffsinger, Church of the Brethren, has now joined this wonderful group!

I can't articulate my gratitude to the people of the Religion Division of the Lilly Endowment, past and present. You have encouraged, counseled, nudged and helped me develop as a pastor since my beginning years in ministry. Your clarity, discernment and heart for the Gospel continues to help the Spirit change our churches. Bob Lynn, Craig Dykstra, Jeanne Knoerle, Jim Wind and Chris Coble: thank you each for your support and wise counsel.

Jacqueline Wenger, Kim Gage Ryan and Kris Tenny-Brittian traveled from Missouri, D.C. and Seattle to spend a week at our cabin to design questionnaires. I think 35 degrees below zero (straight temperature, not wind chill) in a cabin in the lonely, forested reaches of far northern Minnesota in February is paradise itself. However, a few of my friends have suggested that this trip may constitute evidence of extreme devotion to the cause. Huh…

Jackie helped design and oversee the sociological part of the Mainline Evangelism Project with scholarly insight, deep faith and humor. Our full report can be downloaded from ***www. GraceNet.info.*** Kim, my dear pastor friend, has read drafts, mulled ideas, listened, prayed and tested ideas I was forming about practical evangelism. Kris gave two years of her life to this work. She sorted and sifted data, de-glitched new software and vetted footnotes and bibliographies. She visited churches and interviewed pastors, church secretaries and new Christians. Kris has helped me make sense of four years of work on evangelism. Thank you all.

Elizabeth Lang Harman and Sarah Emily Gauche are two brilliant Midwestern pastors' daughters who go to college on opposite coasts. They live in circumstances in which Christianity is viewed with deep suspicion. Each has a fresh perspective on evangelism that we, in the safe confines of middle age and established churches, almost can't imagine. They have done research, kept journals, mulled ideas for hours and read drafts of this book. A third amazing young woman, Sarah Montgomery White, has also shared her strong faith, her insights, her questions and love of serving others. My talks with each of you echoed in my soul as I thought about which things were really important and how to say them clearly. Thank you.

We all have experiences that shape our understanding of life and ministry forever. Two have been particularly important to me. Much of what I understand about churches I learned from Carmel Christian Church (Disciples of Christ), which I served for seven years. Thank you all for everything you taught me. I am so grateful for our time together.

The next great ministry experience was the Bethany Project, a pilot project in congregational revitalization through the spiritual leadership of 150 Disciples of Christ pastors. This book both arises out of the Bethany experience and is a response to it. I will always be grateful to you, Bethany pastors. I wish we could dedicate this book by singing in the Old Meeting House.

Many dear friends have helped me think about faith, church and evangelism during these last years. Thank you each for your insights, your ability to spot the weak point in an argument, your appreciation of a glimmer of truth. You have prayed for this work and for me. Most of you have poured over this manuscript and made wonderful suggestions. The mistakes are mine! Thank you all, more than I can say: Ann Azdell, Liz Bowman, Sherry Brittian, Catherine Caffey, Ellie Campbell, Bob Cornwall, Laura Cuaz, Betsie Czeschin, Pamela Dolan, Beth Dorton, Chuck Denison, Sue Dullard, Kate Dullard, Barry and Patricia Feld, Becky Garrison, Nancy Lee Gauche, Jeff Gill, Jim Griffith, Dick Hamm, Ginny Heisey, Bob Hill, Todd Hunter, Julie Ingstad, Heidi Korstad, Leeann Korstad, Nicole Korstad, Tryna Loos, Jerri Lynn, Malia Mullahey, Paul Scanlon, Patience Schock, Dave Schoen, Nancy Stimson, Gary Straub, Joanne Thomson, Sharon Tutko, Dawn Weaks, Maribeth Blackman Westerfield and Newell Williams.

I am grateful to the people at Chalice Press for all of their work on this book. Wes Buchek, Trent Butler, Pam Brown, Lynne Letchworth, Gail Stobaugh, and Elizabeth Wright—you have been kind, gracious and skillful. Thank you.

Don Schutt has been a partner in ministry for more than 15 years. Each part of this project and book has been shaped by his insights into people, life in Christ, the church, scripture and by his prayer. I have no words. Thank you, Don.

I used to think it was pro forma good manners that prompted authors to thank their spouses for their infinite patience and kindness, endurance of obsessive narcissism, skilled reading of drafts, sweetly worded advice, prayer, supportive critique, encouragement and enticement to long walks and the occasional meal away from the keyboard. I now see that fulsome gratitude falls short of the mark. Thank you, Russ White. You have been a saint—a patient, kind, insightful, brilliant saint; a sparker of creativity; and ballast.

MGR
Wolf Run
Marcell, Minnesota

Series Foreword

What a promising project! Martha Grace Reese's "trilogy" may be the most useful resource for awakening slumbering churches that has come along in a very long time. She publishes it at a critical time in the history of Protestant Christianity in North America. Ninety-nine percent of our mainline churches have little or no effective engagement with people in their communities who are not yet people of faith, hope and love. Unlike their forebears, our churches' main business is no longer "apostolic." We care for "our people"—oblivious to the fact that, due to the secularization of the West, our churches are now placed in the largest mission field in the Western hemisphere (and the third largest mission field on earth).

The **Unbinding the Gospel Series** includes three resources: **Unbinding the Gospel**, **Unbinding Your Heart**, and **Unbinding Your Church**. Each has the "unbinding" metaphor in common. It is an accurate and powerful metaphor. Like Gulliver, who was once tied down by so many small strings he could not move, most mainline churches are so "tied down" by their traditions, customs, routines, assumptions, perceptions, anxieties, passivity, denial, scapegoating, and (yes) rationalizations that they feel powerless to move. And, keep in mind, these churches are in denominations and traditions that were, once upon a time, great contagious movements in this land!

It occurs to me that our need for unbinding extends even beyond Gospel, Heart and Church. For instance, many conventional Christians have binders—or filters—over their eyes. They mistake the masks that people wear for their real faces, so they assume that people are more "okay" than they really are. They wager that pre-Christian people do not really need to experience forgiveness, justification, reconciliation, or second birth; or to experience the grace, love, peace, or Kingdom of God; or to join the Body of Christ; or join God's movement in the world; or to fulfill the will and purpose of God for their lives.

Most church members have bound "tongues" as well. They, tragically, assume that "witnessing" necessarily involves "preaching at" people. They do not want to do that! They do not even **want** to want to do that! Most church people love conversation, however. When they discover that faith-sharing best takes place through conversation, their tongues are often liberated.

Nevertheless, Reese's **Unbinding the Gospel Series** addresses eye and tongue bindings covertly, while addressing the bound heart and church overtly. These books are rooted in Martha Grace Reese's four years of Lilly Endowment-funded research into all kinds of effective evangelism, including a study of the 1% or so of mainline churches that actually reach unchurched people in significant numbers. The work seems to embraces the full range of mainline theology and melts traditional dividing lines. She and her colleagues stand on the shoulders of the Church's evangelical tradition to help churches today to find their way forward. So traditional features like worship, sermons, small groups, prayer, testimony, and narrative play prominent roles in the ***Unbinding the Gospel Series***. Readers will see, however, the imagination and innovation expressed in these expressions.

Some features within these books are new, with little or no precedent. ***Unbinding Your Church***, for instance, has a chapter specifically for church musicians, ***by*** church musicians! I noticed that the project commends resources in Spanish as well as English. I am embarrassed that in the most multilingual nation-state on earth, recognizing any other language than American English will be regarded as avant garde. This reveals the extent to which our churches are pathologically out of touch with the changing mission field around them.

Unbinding Your Church prepares churches for a sustained "E-vent" to catalyze the church into outreach. I expect such E-vents to move at least 20,000 churches into their first invitational foray into the community in anyone's memory. To keep the momentum, they will need to "institutionalize" evangelism as a "regular" ongoing ministry of the People of God. Evangelism—like worship, Christian education, and regular giving—must be institutionalized expressions of our life together. Furthermore, the churches that get really serious will develop a strategic plan for their future mission and growth. They will become local movements through the strategic perspectives featured by the Church Growth movement at its best.

Most important, this whole series focuses on "Real Life Evangelism." Christianity is not only, or even mainly, a fire escape or a ticket to heaven. The faith is a redemptive approach to the whole of our lives—this side of death as well as beyond. I predict that churches whose leaders and people are tired of net membership decline, and tired of slow death by attrition, will take to the ***Unbinding the Gospel Series*** big time. Reese is right that our churches are stuck. By my calculations, at least 200,000 churches in the USA are stuck. Alas, churches cannot get "unstuck" without their full cooperation. This series ***can*** help them regain momentum.

George G. Hunter III
Distinguished Professor of Evangelization and Church Growth
School of World Mission and Evangelism
Asbury Theological Seminary

PART ONE

■ **PART ONE** focuses on *what is* and on *what can be* for individuals and for churches.

■ **PART TWO** helps you see your church more clearly and start to move toward new possibilities.

■ **PART THREE** is your 40-day, individual prayer journal. Use it on your own each day. You can discuss it each week when you meet with your study group.

Wake up, and strengthen what remains. (Rev. 3:2)

Breaking the Curse

October 2004. The country watched as the curse was broken. On the night of a total eclipse, after 86 years of heart-wrenching defeat, Boston fans' cheers ricocheted off the walls of Busch Stadium and ascended into the firmament as the Boston Red Sox won their first World Series since trading Babe Ruth. Ballplayers can be superstitious folks. They believe in things like Lucky Game Underwear that Can't Be Washed or the Winning Streak Will Break. Trading Babe Ruth was a *Bad* Thing for the Red Sox. As the results rolled in, year after year, the fans, the Red Sox Nation knew it. But 86 years later, a miracle happened in St. Louis, and cheers echoed around the world.

About 86 years ago mainline churches did something. Maybe we washed our lucky game underwear. Maybe we traded Babe Ruth. Lots of people have lots of ideas. But we have not been winning any evangelism series for one *looong* stretch of time. It's about time *that* curse gets broken. It can be done. It is time to see *our* players jumping and slapping each other's backs. It is time to hear the cheers of *our* fans echoing into the firmament again. It is time.

This book is about breaking the curse. It's about untying the knots that keep us from living exciting lives in the Spirit. It's about unbinding the Good News that God adores us and everyone else, that God has shown this to us through Jesus Christ. This is a book that is unabashedly about evangelism: faith sharing.

A Book about the E Word

This book is about breaking the curse, untying the knots that keep us from living exciting lives in the Spirit. It's about unbinding the Good News that God adores us and everyone else, that God has shown this to us through Jesus Christ. This book is unabashedly about evangelism: faith sharing. It's intended for members and pastors of churches who want to start living a more exciting life with God and with each other. It's intended for members and pastors of churches who want to share that joy with people who don't know it.

This book is about *evangelism,* the "E" word. The E word seems to have replaced sex and money as That Which Must Not Be Named in our mainline churches! Most of us feel guilty about our losing streak. Sometimes we ignore it. Sometimes we rationalize it. Let's stop that. Instead, let's make some changes in our focus, our training, our lineup and our game plan.

The book you hold in your hands can provide a starting point. It was born from the Mainline Evangelism Project, a four-year study of hundreds of mainline congregations.[1] We interviewed over 1200 church members, new Christians and pastors. We scoured statistics and visited churches. We met with pastors and laypeople, professors and seminarians, denominational officials and kids in the youth group. We conducted a statistical study of the beliefs, motivations and actions of 150 of the mainline churches that are doing the best job reaching people with no church background.[2]

The purpose of the study was to find churches that are doing effective evangelism and to discover their motivations. We also wanted to discover what makes these congregations, their pastors and their members tick. How do they think? What are they doing? We uncovered some painful facts and attitudes. Then we found some exciting answers that hold hope for the rest of us!

The most important result of all our research is that there is great hope for our churches. And our hope is in God.

Our most important discovery is that a vivid relationship with God lies at the heart of real evangelism. People who share their faith love God and believe that other people's lives would be better if they were in a relationship with God, too. They know why they are doing evangelism: they want to share a driving force in their lives. These Christians are growing in their own faith. They learn to talk about it. Their churches put a high priority on evangelism—faith sharing.

Churches that are doing wonderful evangelism have three important things in common:

1. The heart of evangelism is being in love with God, being part of a church you love, and caring about other people who do not live with this faith. Faith sharing focuses on relationships, not "bringing in more young people," or "helping our church to grow again." Evangelism is ***motivated*** by growing love—not by all the lists, bread deliveries, mailings, parties for unchurched friends, cell group curriculum decisions or new members' classes. Details matter. Means

---

This book is about *evangelism,* the "E" word. The E word has replaced sex and money as "That Which Must Not Be Named" in our mainline churches!

The most important result of all our research is that there is great hope for our churches. And our hope is in God.

of showing love are important, but the heart of evangelism is love—of God, of church, of others.

2. People in evangelistic churches can tell you what difference being a Christian makes in their own lives. They believe passionately that having a relationship with God and being part of their church community will help both friends and people they've never met. Many other mainline Christians, along with many mainline pastors, have a hard time articulating how being a Christian matters—for themselves or for anyone else.

3. Key leaders in churches of every theological stripe hold their churches to a laser-like focus on: (a) church members' growing relationships with Christ, and (b) sharing their faith with others.

Vibrant evangelism has no theological bounds. It isn't about talking people into beliefs. It isn't about scaring them with horror stories of Hell. Converted, healed lives do not come about by an intellectual assent to a list of propositions. ("Pray this prayer and you'll go to Heaven," or, "Believe this theological/political agenda and you're in.") There are no quick fixes, no silver bullets. But we *can* change our thinking, and we *can* change our habits!

At its core, evangelism is people sharing with others their personal understandings that life is better, richer, truer if one has faith in Christ and lives in a faith community. These are some of the things that people in churches, many of them quite ordinary churches, are discovering as they begin to share their faith beyond church walls.

Faith sharing changes the lives of Christians who do it. Many Christians in evangelistic churches (and their pastors) volunteered striking experiences. When they started learning to articulate their own faith and to share it with others, they began to see "coincidences," "answers to prayer," "miracles." Life felt different. They were more aware of tiny promptings from the Spirit. They say this new life with the Spirit felt even richer when they started seeing changes in the lives of the people with whom they talked about their faith. They never want to go back to the old days of mute, and muted, faith.

One pastor said, "I used to preach and run the church. After the accident, I started talking with people about what really matters in my own life. After I had experienced a tragedy and recovered a bit, I wanted to at least listen to other people about whatever situation they're in. This has given me a feeling of being more in touch with God and of being a more 'full-time' Christian instead of a maintenance pastor. Talking about faith one-on-one and working with the church on it has become completely addictive. As addictions go, it's a great one!"

> Converted, healed lives do not come about by an intellectual assent to a list of propositions. There are no quick fixes, no silver bullets. But we *can* change our thinking, and we *can* change our habits!

Our Context for Faith Sharing

You may be a member of a church that is smaller than it was in 1950 or 1960. Many older members remember wonderful days of citywide Fifth Sunday hymn sings and huge community Thanksgiving services. Things are smaller now. Many churches have fewer young families, fewer children, and lower budgets. Furnaces are older, bathrooms antique. People say, "You know, it's not just happening to our church; this is happening to everyone." Not all churches are shrinking, but that statement has a lot of truth to it. It's *not* just your church. The whole country has changed. Let's take a brief look at the context in which God has called us to share our faith so we can see our situation clearly. (If you are a fact and statistics hound, please read the first book in the ***Unbinding the Gospel Series—Unbinding the Gospel,***[3] and go to **www.GraceNet.info**) If you don't like statistics at all, skip or skim the rest of this chapter. Really!

The heart of evangelism is having an alive relationship with God, being part of a church you love and caring that people outside the church find what you've discovered.

Does Faith Sharing Intimidate Us? Yes. The most comprehensive study of congregational pastors revealed that most pastors love being in ministry. It also showed that pastors' greatest discouragement is that they feel ineffectual sharing the Gospel in this culture ("Duke Study").[4] Many laypeople concur. In an extensive study, church members ranked faith sharing/evangelism as the very weakest link in a list of 54 things their churches do![5]

Have the Mainline Denominations Lost Members? Yes. The seven mainline denominations in our study declined from 26 million to 21 million members between 1960 and 2000, a decline of almost 20%.[6] That's not good. But the picture dims when we realize that the U.S. population has grown.[7] These denominations have gone from making up 14.4% of the American population to only 7.4%. In percentage terms, in the year 2000 there were only half as many mainline Protestants as there were 40 years before.

Is the Protestant Presence in the U.S. Declining? Yes. Recent research from the University of Chicago shows that America's Protestant majority is gone.[8] From 1972 until 1993, the percentage of Protestants in the U.S. remained fairly stable at about 63%. However, by 2002 the number had dropped to 50%. It is now substantially below that. Protestants are in steady decline.

Is America Becoming a Less Religious Country? Yes. Only 4% of people who were born in the U.S. between 1910 and 1919 say they have no religious preference. That number rises to 27% of those born 1980 and 1984. Each generation is less involved in religious life than the one that came before it.[9]

Our big picture diagnosis for the church is that the whole country is getting more complicated and, in many ways, more interesting! We have more types of people, with different racial, cultural and religious backgrounds, than we did 50 years ago. Children are being born to parents who have no faith tradition whatsoever. One hundred years ago you would have had to search hard to find someone who didn't know the Christmas story. Today all we have to do is walk into the local high school.

In 1960, pews filled when a loving, well-run church opened its doors. Today, people who have never attended a church populate our neighborhoods and work places. The next decades will see millions more. They won't have memories of a Christian grandmother, father or next-door neighbor. The thought of "going back to church" when they're in trouble will never occur to them, because they have never been inside a church building in the first place. For them, a church is an alien, possibly intimidating place—not a cradle of comfort and hope.

We used to be able to share the faith easily because just being part of our country took care of some of the beginning parts of evangelism. That's happening less and less. Have you ever said, "I don't talk to people about religion because people need to make their own choices about what they believe?" Think about it. Right or wrong, we have relied on just being American to teach people about Christianity. Those days of passive absorption are ending. We now have to do more of the beginning work of educating people about the faith, or we will rob millions of people of the option of being Christian. Is that a shocking thought?

We must make organized, conscious, coordinated efforts to change our reliance on "passive absorption" of the faith. If we want people to understand or enter a faith life, we have to figure out ways to share our faith. Now.

How Well Are Mainline Churches Helping New People Become Christians? Very Badly. The main focus of the Mainline Evangelism Project was to find examples of mainline churches that are doing effective jobs of evangelism, to try to figure out what makes them tick and to share what we learned with other churches interested in doing more effective evangelism. In the process of doing that, we discovered:

- New Christians are joining the faith in the mainline churches, but the vast majority are our own children or new spouses.
- 65% to 80% of the fastest-growing congregations in each denomination are in the South or are predominantly racial/

Highlight Findings of the Mainline Evangelism Project

1. If we know ***why*** to do evangelism, we'll figure out ***how*** to do it.

2. Faith sharing arises out of vibrant relationships with God.

3. It is important to learn to talk about our faith.

4. Where it flourishes, evangelism is a high priority for pastor, congregation and individuals.

ethnic. (All but one of these denominations range from 88% to 97% Caucasian.) This minority of congregations is responsible for about three quarters of our best evangelism.

■ If the good evangelism statistics of southern churches and racial/ethnic churches are excluded, we found that only ½ of 1% of 30,000 mainline churches studied were doing a significant job reaching unchurched people,[10] measured by an average of five adult baptisms a year.

■ Whole generations of mainline pastors have little training and virtually no personal experience of vivid, joyous faith sharing. In 72 mainline seminaries, only 8 require even half a course in evangelism for graduation with an ordination degree. (The half course is usually combined with stewardship!!! How's that for a meal of lima beans and liver?)[11]

In percentage terms, in the year 2000 there were only half as many mainline Protestants as there were 40 years before.

These are overwhelming statistics. We ignore this Good Friday news at our peril.

Signs of Hope

But there's also good news:

Old Congregations Are Reaching Unchurched People. Here is the first green leaf dropped by a dove into the office of the Mainline Evangelism Project. How long do you think the 150 congregations performing all those adult baptisms have been in existence? The accepted wisdom is that new churches can reach unchurched people most effectively. That lets the rest of us in all our old churches off the hook, right? Wrong!

We found something very different. Our high adult baptism congregations ranged in age from 4 to 270 years! The median age of our high baptism congregations was 96 years old. The average age was 89 years. (Median age means that half of the congregations surveyed were younger than 96 and half were older.) It is now clear: a congregation may be too stuck in its ways to do evangelism, but it's not too old! That's an exciting thought.

A Change Coming: Three Signs

We may be on the leading edge of a change. These indicators of shifts are not yet widespread, but they are clear.

1. Mainline pastors and laypeople are beginning to see and say out loud that they are not doing a good job with evangelism. It bothers them! Insight helps.

2. Some of the old liberal/conservative/charismatic polarizations are beginning to shift and melt. With that is coming a deeper spiritual/prayer life and more attention to scripture for many mainline pastors. Spiritual disciplines often free up a desire to share their faith. In effective, small-scale ways, we are starting to learn things people in other parts of Christ's church already know.

3. After decades of little or no activity in new church planting and evangelism, some denominations, synods and churches are shifting their priorities. Some sectors of the church are beginning to grow.

The Spirit Seems to Be Doing Something.

Let's say this right out loud. The Spirit of God seems to be doing something in mainline churches. I am rarely accused of wearing rose-colored contacts. However, after years of working with pastors and denominational leaders, I recognize a pattern of movement toward life and health and an overflowing of the Gospel in the mainline church. We can choose to focus on the same old treadmill of church maintenance. We can choose to be paralyzed by the grief of institutional decline. We can get angry about a lack of vision and power that many experienced during the Civil Rights movement of the '60s and in social justice work in the '70s. But these may not be the threads to follow out of this particular labyrinth.

The scale is small, but new things are happening!

This is the good news: There is a God. And large numbers of pastors, church members, elders, deacons, vestries, sessions, heads of church councils and evangelism committees, synods, regions and entire denominations stand ready to open their minds and hearts to the idea of unbinding the knots with which we've trussed the Gospel. Significant numbers of us appear willing to change and learn new things. We are putting ourselves on the line and putting resources—time, energy, money, prayer and focus—behind the efforts. Our efforts are bearing some fruit.

As the pastor of a now rapidly growing American Baptist church said, "You know, it almost doesn't matter where you start with evangelism. God has blessed some pretty halting, stumbling efforts we've made. Maybe when it comes to sharing the Gospel we just need to jump in from whatever point on the shore we're standing and start paddling around."

One hundred years ago you would have had to search hard to find someone who didn't know the Christmas story. Today all we have to do is walk into the local high school.

We don't even think about the importance of community service. We just help out with the Kiwanis Club, the Boy Scout troop, the symphony. Who knows how many of the things we "just do" come from having been raised in a country that has been overwhelmingly Christian and Protestant? That is changing, and no one knows the results to come. We may be feeling the leading edge of the change by seeing how much harder it is to do evangelism.

A Big Thank You...Names...and Stories. Over 1200 people spoke honestly with us about deep feelings and understandings of their faith. Thank you to each of you. I quote many people and describe many churches. The geographic and denominational descriptions are accurate. I have changed people's and congregations' names. Where a full name is given for a person, it is a real name. I have masked the identities of the few negative examples more heavily. Quotations are accurate, although I have simplified some sentences and clarified some grammar. A few of the long quotes are compilations of basic stories that we heard again and again. However, each of the three stories in chapter 4 is accurate to a particular church—they are not compilations.

How to use this book. Please use the steps outlined in the Unbinding the Gospel Series two-page description at the beginning of this book. *Unbinding Your Heart* has an individual prayer exercise for each day of your six-week group study. Read the introduction and first chapter the first week. Each chapter lists questions and an exercise for your group to use each week. There is way too much to discuss in an hour. Please do spend at least the first ten minutes of each group session talking about what is happening in your individual prayer. (See *Unbinding Your Church: Pastor's and Leaders' Guide* for detailed class suggestions.) Your leader and the group can choose which questions or exercises you will do each week. There's only one rule: enjoy your group time and dare to think and do new things!

Let's Get Started!

We have heard stories of inspiration, struggle, excitement, disappointment, spiritual learning and changes in lives and churches for four years. We found no rigid formula for success, no magic plan that will work for every church. Each individual must enter the great adventure by thinking, learning more, praying, and asking God a humble question: "Which small things can I do today to help more people know you?"

This adventure may take you on a trip you can't anticipate. You may have to pack a bag and go far. The Boston Red Sox won the Series in St. Louis—not before the home crowd at Fenway Park.

Are you ready to get going?

---

[1]The Mainline Evangelism Study, made possible by a grant from the Lilly Endowment, Inc., studied congregations in seven denominations over a period of four years: American Baptist Churches USA, Christian Church (Disciples of Christ), Evangelical Lutheran Church in America, Presbyterian Church USA, Reformed Church in America, United Church of Christ and The United Methodist Church.

[2]See www.GraceNet.info for a formal sociological report on this survey.

[3]Martha Grace Reese, *Unbinding the Gospel: Real Life Evangelism* (St. Louis: Chalice Press, 2007).

[4]See the Survey of Clergy at www.pulpitandpew.duke.edu/research.html.

[5]Homeland Ministries and Church Extension Faithful Planning Congregational Survey Results, 2001-2005.

[6]All calculations for these figures are as conservative, simple and realistic as we could make them. Four of the denominations have had mergers between 1960 and 2000, so we added together the denominational figures for the merging churches at the beginning. In two cases, a sizeable number of churches left the denomination. We have taken those churches (the Lutheran Church Missouri Synod and the Independent Christian Churches and Churches of Christ) out of the numbers from the beginning, so they never show up in these tables. So, for example, the Evangelical and Reformed churches are counted as part of the UCC numbers in 1960, even though the merger between the E & R and the Congregational Christian Churches hadn't yet occurred. The Missouri Synod Lutherans and the Independent Christian Churches are not listed in 1960 figures for the ELCA and the DOC even though they were counted in denominational numbers at the time. Our intent is to show only true decline, since no one would make the case that Missouri Synod Lutherans or Independent Christians are lost to the Kingdom! Our figures are compiled from the American Religion Data Archive at www.thearda.com/Denoms/Family.

[7]Population figures are from the U.S. Census, 1960 and 2000, http://www.census.gov/prod/2002pubs/censr-4.pdf.

[8]The University of Chicago's National Opinion Research Center (NORC) published a study in July 2004 called "The Vanishing Protestant Majority." The principal author of the study is Tom W. Smith, who is also Director of NORC's General Social Survey, one of the most scientifically reliable gauges of public trends. For details or full text of the study, see www.norc.uchicago.edu., Tom W. Smith and Seokho Kim, "The Vanishing Protestant Majority," *GSS Social Change Report* No. 49 (NORC/University of Chicago, July 2004), 21 (http://www.norc.uchicago.edu/issues/PROTSG08.pdf.

[9]These conclusions are drawn from the University of Chicago study, ibid.

[10]We did not count "re-baptisms," and the total number of baptisms over the three-year period had to be larger than 1% of average worship attendance. We found significant denominational record-keeping differences, mistakes in record-keeping and data entry, and theological differences between infant and believers' baptisms and "re-baptisms." We made the lists as comparable as possible and verified congregational statistics with hundreds of phone calls to congregational record keepers and pastors. Although United Methodist congregations were called, interviewed and participated in the survey, they are not included in the pool of 30,000 congregations because they do not keep distinct adult baptism records. For a more complete report of the survey results and our judgment calls to correlate and verify data, please see the Mainline Evangelism Project report by Jacqueline E. Wenger with Martha Grace Reese and J. Kristina Tenny-Brittian at http://www.GraceNet.info.

[11]These data were collected in 2005 and 2006 by phone calls to seminaries.

Right or wrong, we have relied on just being American to teach people about Christianity. Those days of passive absorption are ending. We now have to do more of the beginning work of educating people about the faith, or we will rob millions of people of the option of being Christian.

CHAPTER 1

Why <u>Do</u> Evangelism?

WHY Do Evangelism?

Let's start at the pivot point. Why did you pick up this book? Why does evangelism matter? Right now, will you stop reading and write down the first thoughts that come to mind?

We made a surprising discovery during our four-year study of mainline evangelism. A huge number of mainline church members and pastors feel awkward, embarrassed, uncomfortable, defensive or angry when evangelism is mentioned. We believe that most mainline members, pastors and denominational ministers would rather not think too much about evangelism. Christian book publishers have said that a book with the word *evangelism* in the title is death at the box office! So you are in a special minority to be reading this book at all. What motivates *you*?

We found that most mainline Christians who are doing successful evangelism are motivated by two things: a love of their church and a living relationship with God. Now, *many* of us love our churches and have a living relationship with God. Why aren't we all doing significant evangelism? One reason is simple. We haven't focused on it for decades. Evangelism has drifted into a side stream of our attention, in denominations, in seminaries, and in most congregations' preaching and teaching. We now have generations of pastors who have little or no training in evangelism. Worse, many pastors have no positive, personal experience with evangelism. And evangelism isn't cool. One pastor said, "Why don't I do evangelism? Do you want me to be really honest? Doing evangelism wouldn't help me get along with my pastoral peers. And I'd look like one of those naive, earnest, sort of scruffy guys to our bishop."

What Is Evangelism?

For this book, evangelism is anything you do to help another person move closer to a relationship with God, or into Christian community.

13

Lack of inspiring emphasis on evangelism in our pastors' backgrounds and training both reflects the mainline churches' feelings about evangelism and reinforces such feelings for the next generation. Lack of training and personal experience—in their churches growing up, in seminary, and in peer relationships as congregational pastors— contribute to ministerial frustrations related to evangelism. Remember? American pastors say their greatest frustration in ministry is their inability to convey the Gospel in this culture (Duke Study). If pastors aren't excited about evangelism, it is unlikely that their parishioners will be. I believe that our pastors' experiential vacuum explains why church members identify key pieces of evangelism as their congregations' two weakest links (Disciples Members' Survey; see the introduction).

> Our churches are made up of the "evangelism lovers" and the "evangelism-cautious!" The majority hear the word *evangelism* and begin to feel queasy. They back quietly toward the door, trying not to attract attention as they slip silently from the room.

We did discover heartening new developments in the study, but decades of inattention to an inspiring evangelism that fits mainline theology have consequences we will live with for a long time. Evangelism in our churches is like a yellow Lego™ piece that skidded unseen under the refrigerator one hot July afternoon. By the time moving day rolls around four years later, that little Lego™ has collected more fuzzy dust and dog hair than ***anyone*** wants to look at!

So what dust has our Lego,™ evangelism, collected during these years of snoozing quietly under the church's refrigerator? To begin to understand this, let's look at three areas:

1. What do we think when we hear the word *"evangelism"*?
2. What difference does it make if people are Christians? and
3. What motivates us to share the Gospel?

What Do We Think When We Hear the Word Evangelism?

The biggest predicament we face in relation to evangelism involves our emotions! We talked with over 1200 laypeople and pastors about evangelism during the Mainline Evangelism Project. We asked both individuals and groups: "What do you think about when you hear the word *'evangelism'?*" Typical first-impression answers included:

- ■ "No! I don't want to knock on strangers' doors and give them some pamphlet."
- ■ "A televangelist is asking for money for the theme park."
- ■ "Our pastor gives this boring, annual, muddled sermon (in a slooow, deep, stained-glass voice) that 'evangelism is pointing out the laden table to a hungry man,' whatever ***that*** means."

- "My college roommate kept hammering me about salvation and trying to talk me into giving my life to Christ."
- "I cringe at the memories from the years when *I* pummeled people with those embarrassing questions about salvation! I don't believe in Hell now. I think people should make up their own minds, without pressure."
- "I don't even want to *think* about evangelism. We're doing a bad job and we've tried."
- "I know we're *supposed* to talk with people about faith and invite them to church, but I don't want to lose friends. I feel guilty."
- "I don't think we *should* do evangelism—it implies other religions are wrong."

Many of the cartoonish evangelistic pictures in our heads are caricatures of bad practices.

After this book was sent to the publisher, long after I had called evangelism "the E word," I discovered that the United Church of Christ's "God Is Still Speaking" campaign uses the phrase, "the e.word." Another confirmation! Those of us who are trying to do it in the mainline churches all figure out, sooner or later, that "evangelism" is not a good out-loud word! And then, after almost losing hope, the one person in ten will say:

- "I had this amazing experience last year with a friend at work who came to know Christ because of our friendship. It was *incredible!*"

Evangelism Lovers and the Evangelism-Cautious

Some mainline church people *don't* have strong feelings about evangelism, but they represent a small minority! The Mainline Evangelism Project uncovered a Great Divide in the way our church people, pastors and denominational ministers feel about evangelism. After years of conversations, in my mind's eye I see two groups of people, poised on opposite banks of a chasm that opens up in the middle of the living room when the "E" bomb is dropped into a conversation! Almost everyone is on one side of that great divide or the other. A minority of people in mainline churches are passionate about the importance of evangelism and love sharing their faith with others. The majority hear the word *evangelism* and begin to feel queasy as they back quietly toward the door, trying not to attract attention as they slip from the room.

The Evangelism Lovers

Theology, education, and financial status seem to matter little in determining on which side of this chasm you land. People who share the Gospel as a pattern in their lives, as a spiritual practice, love to think about it and talk about it. They remember specific conversations with people they care about. They call up pictures of time spent in prayer for friends. They have stories of lives that were changed because someone is now a Christian and has a deep sense of meaning and community.

They tell of a man who gave his life to Christ. He is now sober and cares for his family. They talk about a woman disillusioned by a hypocritical church. Now she loves being an elder in their congregation. They tell about a gay couple who have gained a church home. They think of high school kids, off drugs, who have something to work for and people to lean into as they face the challenges teenagers encounter. They have memories of a businesswoman who was isolated and bitter. Now she has organized a ministry to feed homeless people with extra food from restaurants and grocery stores. They tell of a 70-year-old who came to grips with questions about God that had haunted him since he was in high school and his father died. People who share their faith talk about Jesus (if they're theologically liberal, they tend to talk about Christ) and about their relationships with him. They talk about God teaching them more each day.

The Evangelism-Cautious

Now, what does evangelism feel like for most pastors and people in mainline congregations? The very word can push buttons that carry a 220 current! We asked groups of church folks to call out words that the term "evangelism" brings to mind. The air was full of only half-laughing shouts like "pushy," "embarrassing," "uncomfortable," "going to Hell," "awkward," "tracts," "pressuring," "Tammy Faye Bakker," "Bible thumpers," and "Don't **talk** about it—I don't even want to **think** about this!"

After a while, interview discussions tended to center on questions and opinions like, "How can I do evangelism when I believe that many paths lead to God?" "Why do I think I know enough to tell someone what to believe?" "I love God, but I'm uncomfortable with the people who do evangelism. I don't think they're expressing authentic Lutheran (Presbyterian, Disciple, UCC, Methodist, Episcopalian, Reformed Church, American Baptist) theology." "What if someone asked a question I don't know the answer to?" "If a congregation really focuses on evangelism, it doesn't do much with justice issues or deal with the systemic effects of racism." And, "I don't want to alienate my friends."

> Evangelism is no panacea. A conversion moment is a *moment*, and a life with Christ continues for years of ups and downs, of "little conversions."

The evangelism lovers and the evangelism-cautious paint vastly different pictures of evangelism. One is beautiful—it could be an idyllic painting of a mother and daughters by impressionist Mary Cassatt. The second painting is perhaps by Edvard Munch (he painted *The Scream,* which looks the way it sounds and raises the hairs on the back of your neck). These portraits by the evangelism lovers and the evangelism-cautious are both accurate to some degree, but neither captures the full faith landscape.

Evangelism lovers tend to concentrate on the glorious high spots of a life of sharing their faith. They talk about what motivates them. In their enthusiasm, they don't always tell about the teenagers who drift away, the dad who starts drinking again, the depressed 70-year-old's bad days. Evangelism is not a panacea. A conversion moment is a *moment,* and a life with Christ continues for years of ups and downs, of "little conversions."

On the other hand, the evangelism-cautious frequently are living with fears of coercive misuses of evangelism. These fears can stunt one's spiritual life. If our faith is real, if being a Christian makes a deep difference in our own lives, it matters that we be able to talk about that with the people we care about and the people that Christ cares about. Many of the cartoonish evangelistic pictures in our heads are caricatures of bad practices. Some of these ideas are slanted or simply wrong (for example, the thought that evangelism has to do with arguing people into believing they're going to Hell if they don't choose Christ, or the prejudice that evangelism doesn't go together with service to the poor or deep commitments to justice issues.)

> People who have grown up in the church think of Christianity like breathing. You just ***do*** it, you just ***are*** it! This is the downside of growing up nurtured by the church. It's hard to have perspective on what a life ***without*** faith would feel like.

Many of these emotions are unconscious. They are the fuzz and dust on the under-the-refrigerator Lego.™ Why should the fact that some people do a bad job of evangelism stop us from sharing our faith? It shouldn't! During the study discussions and conversations, we discovered an exciting thing. The emotional fuzz and dust can be washed off evangelism if we will:

- look at our feelings about evangelism,
- think about why it matters that *we* are Christian, and
- get a grasp of why it could matter that *other* people become Christians.

What Difference Does Being a Christian Make in Your Own Life?

If you ask most mainline church people why they are (or should be) doing evangelism, they answer, "So that people will join our church." Sometimes they say, "We need more people [young families, children] in our church." This is a secondary focus. I suspect this secondary focus contributes directly to the malaise in our beloved churches. Too often, we slip into treating church like a club. Then our faith slides into thinking first about *church*—about the building, the activities, the friends, the important life we've found there, the ministries we do. We know these ministries can lead to faith in God, a faith life, a prayer life. But we wait too long for the *church* part of a Christian life to lead up to the *God* part of faith. Both are important, but we emphasize the less crucial of the two.

God matters more than church. The purpose of evangelism is to help new men, women and children begin a life of relationship with God. Church supports that relationship. Going to church is not an end in itself. Our failure to focus on our relationship with God has mixed us up. We have let secondary church slide into God's primary place.

The idea for the Mainline Evangelism Project can probably be dated to one conversation I had with some of my favorite people. I was leading a retreat for eight smart, loving pastors of growing mainline churches. Off the cuff, I asked, "Hey, what difference does it make in your *own* life that you are a Christian?"

Silence. *Loud* silence stretched on. And on. I stared around the circle in disbelief. Finally one volunteered hesitantly, "Because it makes me a better person???"

That question hadn't been intended as a pop final. I was not raised in the church, so I have a very clear sense of having made a choice to become a Christian that went against the culture in which I had always lived. I have a good sense of what it is like to be Christian and what it is like *not* to be Christian. Most Christians and most pastors grew up in the church. They did not change cultures to get there.

That silent minute crystallized my understanding that people who have grown up in the church think of their Christianity like breathing. Being Christian is so natural you don't really think about it. You just *do* it, you just *are* it! This is the big downside of growing up nurtured by the church. You think the church *is* the culture. Unless you think about it hard, you assume everyone thinks the way church people do. It's hard to have much perspective on what a life without faith would feel like. So it's hard to help others see what faith would add to their lives.

Since that retreat, I have asked hundreds of pastors what difference being a Christian makes in their own lives. Most reacted

"You know, if we had any *idea* what being a Christian really was, we'd walk around every day feeling like Martians!"

to the question with surprise. Most had a hard time answering. The study revealed a clear difference between typical mainline pastors and pastors who are leading successful evangelistic churches. The "evangelistic pastors" have more complete, integrated, and faster answers to the question.

What Faith Can Be

One Ash Wednesday morning, my ash-crossed forehead prompted three comments at the supermarket (including "Oh, you've got some dirt on your forehead," from a clueless clerk). I mentioned this to one of my wonderful seminary professors, who replied, "You know, if we had any *idea* what being a Christian really was, we'd walk around every day feeling like Martians!"

Annie Dillard wrote, "Does anyone have the foggiest idea of what sort of power we so blithely invoke? Or, as I suspect, does no one believe a word of it? The churches are children playing on the floor with their chemistry sets, mixing up a batch of TNT to kill a Sunday morning. It is madness to wear ladies' straw hats and velvet hats to church; we should all be wearing crash helmets. Ushers should issue life preservers and signal flares; they should lash us to our pews."[1] With that perspective, here's the question: ***What difference does it make in your life that you are a Christian?***

We only dabble our toes at the edges of the waters of faith. Few of us have a clue how vivid and powerful life with Christ can be.

Say It in Words

Here's the next big step. If your faith is already vibrant and alive, can you talk about it? That's the challenge. I was at a friend's house when her toddler threatened to hurl himself out of his high chair. Stretching out a yard-long arm, he shrieked "uhh…Uhh, UHH, UUUHHHHH," as he grabbed for the Cheerios™ in her hand. Sue murmured sweetly, "Say it in ***words,*** Mac."

Well, if we want evangelistic Cheerios,™ if we want to help people discover the joys of being a Christian, we're going to have to learn to say it in words! What's at the heart of life with God? A powerful relationship between each one of us and the Trinity. A powerful relationship between each one of us and other Christians, all of us together helping to bear Christ to those who don't know him. Now let's learn to say it in words. Knowing it and saying it—that's the heart of evangelism.

Faith Quiz

Do you say yes to any of the following statements?

1. I'm living a faith that doesn't make me buckle my seatbelt when I reach for my Bible in the mornings.

2. I'm living without Christ guiding me through the meetings, conversations and choices of my day.

3. I don't feel a deep sense of repentance or forgiveness.

4. I am seldom aware of leadings from the Spirit.

If you answer yes to any of these questions, please, ***please*** ask God to help you find a book, a group, a church, a friend who will help you take the next step in a richer faith life. There's more. You haven't yet seen some of the glorious horizons of faith.

Does It Matter That Other People Are Christians?
The Motivation to Share Your Faith

Great evangelism arises out of vivid faith lives. It occurs all along the theological spectrum. The reasons people articulate for why their own faith is important to them are powerful—and personal. But to do evangelism we must take the next step. We must go beyond ourselves and our faith lives. We must reach out to others. We must *speak* to others! Why does it matter that other people become Christians? When we know *why* it matters to be Christian, we will learn to talk about it. We're smart people. When we know *why* it matters to be Christian, we will figure out *how* to help others begin lives of faith.

God is more important than church. The purpose of evangelism is to help new men, women and children begin a life of relationship with God. Church supports that relationship. Going to church is not an end in itself. Our failure to focus on our relationship with God has mixed us up. We have let secondary church slide into God's primary place.

The move from our own feelings and experience of faith to evangelism involves motivation, a sense of importance, of urgency. Barbara Tuchman, the popular historian, wrote, "With all its problems, Israel has one commanding advantage: a sense of purpose. Israelis may not have affluence…or the quiet life. But they have what affluence tends to smother: a motive."[2] One thing is certain. Like national existence for the Israelis, unless we have a clear motivation to hold the evangelism banners high, they will slip into the dust.

Motivation for sharing faith is the one area in which we found a significant difference between people with conservative and progressive theologies. People across the theological spectrum have deep, personal relationships with God. People across the theological spectrum have reverence for scripture and live in it as the life-giving Word it is. The difference lies in two related areas:

1. biblical belief that the decision to become a Christian is a decision that has eternal consequences (a literal Heaven or Hell upon death) and

2. education and peer support for doing evangelism.

Generally, the more toward the evangelical/conservative side of the spectrum, the greater one's motivation to do evangelism because of Heaven or Hell. Generally, the more evangelical the training, the greater education and peer support for doing evangelism.

One evangelistic mainline pastor spoke with me on the phone for well over an hour. Halfway through the conversation, he began to speak from the depths:

Ok, so there I was, raised in a fundamentalist church, ordained at 21, served churches until I was 29, and my wife left me. Even though the divorce was not my "fault" according to church order, my denomination removed me from serving a congregation for a minimum of two years. My pastor friends and I had a really hard time staying connected. I didn't fit categories and I threatened them. I was ashamed and a wreck. A friend in my apartment complex was a mainline seminary student. He and his wife and their friends were so loving. They included me, prayed with me, listened to me for hours on end, and finally drew me into a part of the church I had always looked at with suspicion.

Long story short, I became part of a mainline denomination, and you don't find people much more progressive biblically than I am now. I haven't believed or preached that people are going to Hell for 30 years. The theological freedom and the grace of this church still amaze me. But I'll tell you, there is one thing that was really hard for me to adjust to. I couldn't believe—I STILL can't believe—how the liberal church that knows so much about God's grace doesn't understand the power of what it has to share. And they don't share it!

I grew up with sword drills and living in the Word,[3] praying every day and training to witness to people about God's offer of salvation. I have years of training that pushes me to care enough for people outside the church to lay my life down for them to help them know Christ. Now I live in this wonderful mainline church. I can't believe so many of my friends don't have the drive to share the Gospel. They've shown the Gospel to me, but they don't share it with strangers. It's Gospel constipation!

I know evangelism was drilled into me when I was young. I know most of my normal mainline colleagues haven't been trained in it. I know 30 years ago when I went to [my fairly typical mainline] seminary if some new student brought up evangelism, people smiled tolerantly and sneaked looks to see where he'd parked his tractor. It didn't take us long to get quiet!

It isn't just the pastors. The other piece of it is that the typical laypeople in my congregations with mainline backgrounds are hesitant to talk about their faith. Most haven't had a lot of experience with prayer or scripture. Talking about God in any very personal way is foreign to them. Once they are exposed to some retreats and prayer groups, Bible studies with real sharing, they're fine. No, more than fine! A lot of them catch fire.

"I think most mainline pastors don't connect their great theology and biblical interpretation with a real experience of God. It's the converts like me—with my background, training and prayer disciplines—who appreciate the strengths of the mainline church the most. The old evangelicals like me are also the ones to look at the church and sound like the girls in our high school youth group, 'Like, wow, totally, can't you guys pull it together?'"

—mainline pastor raised in fundamentalist church

I think most mainline pastors don't connect their great theology and biblical interpretation with a real experience of God. It's the converts like me—with my background, training and prayer disciplines—who appreciate the strengths of the mainline church the most. The old evangelicals like me are also the ones to look at the church and sound like the girls in our high school youth group, "Like, wow, totally, can't you guys pull it together?"

This pastor articulated the heart of our mainline churches' predicament. For decades, most of our seminaries and churches have radically downplayed Hell, the classic motivator for evangelism. Interfaith dialogue has increased the mainline church's sense that many paths lead to God and that we should not bombastically insist on Christianity, or on our particular version of Christianity as the only right faith life. It is interesting that frequently the people who know the most about other religions feel the most comfortable doing Christian evangelism.[4] At the same time, training pastors (and consequently laypeople in congregations) in evangelism has dwindled alarmingly in the last 50 years. No wonder mainline pastors don't know what to share!

> When we know *why* it matters to be Christian, we'll figure out *how* to help other people enter the faith.

The theology most mainline pastors preach is grace-filled. Where that grace is supported by a vivid sense of relationship with Christ, it is real and rich. THIS is what we share! It is important. The good news is that we can share our faith. God exists. We have hope. How do we start?

The Mainline Evangelism Project has demonstrated that churches of all theologies can do exciting, effective evangelism. What matters is having a living relationship with God, being able to talk about it, and church leadership that maintains a laser-like focus on evangelism. Here is a way that may be helpful to analyze your own motivation and your congregation's motivation to do evangelism:

The Gospel Overflowing: The Motivation to Share Your Faith with Others

All right, let's say you know why being a Christian makes a difference in your own life. ***How could being a Christian matter in someone else's life?*** If you care about other people, think about how it could help someone to become Christian, to have a much more conscious relationship with God, and to be a part of Christ's body, the church. There are MANY reasons that being a Christian could help someone. Before you read further, which ones come to mind first?

Traditional American evangelism, true to our national individualism, has put strong emphasis on choice and personal responsibility. Classic teaching stresses that each individual's choice—to be Christian or not to be Christian—decides whether the individual will spend eternity with Christ in Heaven or without Christ, in Hell. Do you believe this? Why or why not? Many people in mainline churches say that they "sort of" believe it, but haven't heard much about it in sermons, so they don't really know. Fair enough. (But not good enough! Don't stop there!) We in the mainline churches are supposed to be such clear, logical thinkers, but our thinking is fuzzy in this area. This fuzziness affects our evangelism. This is a critically important question that we should not gloss over. What do *you* believe? Why?

Evangelism is of massive importance if an eternity in Heaven or Hell is the consequence of the choice to become Christian. If you love people, it matters where they spend eternity. This is a huge motivator.

If you don't believe that becoming a Christian saves you from Hell, what reasons do you have to do evangelism? What else could motivate you to help other people become Christians? These are a few of the more typical reasons people name:

- "A relationship with Christ makes life make sense—it's true."
- "I love God so much I want people to know this joy."
- "Being in a church community gives you a way to serve others and keep growing."
- "Jesus told us to do evangelism in the Great Commission."
- "Life with the Spirit is exciting."
- "I used to be so afraid—with my church and with God, I'm learning to trust."
- "As a Christian, you're part of something important that lasts forever."
- "Children need to learn about God. Parents need help raising kids."
- "I used to feel so guilty about things I had done. Christ has forgiven me, and my church friends love me. I want to help others now."
- "God healed me with a miracle. I want other people to know it's possible."
- "Being with Christ has changed my life from addictions to learning acceptance and grace."

The more important your faith is to you, the more you want to share it. We have hundreds of reasons to share our faith. But the

> The theology most mainline pastors preach is grace-filled. Where that grace is supported by a vivid sense of relationship with Christ, it is real and rich. *THIS* is what we have to share.

reasons have to be real enough to us that we actually say them out loud.

Imagine that you are like a pitcher. You'll only share your faith when you are filled up with reasons and motivations to help other people with their spiritual lives. If you believe that Hell or Heaven is a consequence of a decision to become or not become a Christian, that may fill your pitcher almost to the top! If you don't believe that, you have to have your pitcher filled with many other reasons to get it to the top. Here's a drawing of a pitcher. It has to be overflowing before we share our faith. What is filling your pitcher? Is it overflowing?

Think about the level of your pitcher at other points in your life. Where was it when you first became a Christian? Where was it when you were 17? when you had a child? when you were going through a divorce? when you lost your job? when you attended the most wonderful church service you've ever been to? when someone you loved died? when you moved to a new town? when someone you cared about got the diagnosis?

Churches across the theological spectrum can do exciting, effective evangelism. The crucial factors are living relationships with God, the ability to talk about our faith and church leadership that maintains a laser-like focus on evangelism.

What Motivates You to Share Your Faith?

Our "pitchers," this image of how motivated we are to share our faith, can be filled up by growing faith, by thinking about other people, by encouraging each other to learn how to talk about our faith, by talking about what we believe. But our pitchers can be drained! How?

■ by feeling made fun of,
■ by thoughts that it's wrong or strange to do evangelism,

- by ideas that you're supposed to know answers to any question that might come up,
- by fear of risking a friendship.

Just imagining these negative thoughts about sharing your faith can drain you of motivation!

What's at stake in evangelism is transformed lives, yours included! You and your church can begin to work together on something that matters tremendously. Here is how some people who are sharing their faith talk about it:

- "I love to see people's lives change."
- "I can't tell you what it felt like to see my sister baptized after all those years and all the tough things she had gone through. It was like a new start. I really understood in the Bible then about being 'born again.' That's what happened to [Mary]. She *was* reborn and her life has been a lot better since."
- "I started inviting people to church and they became Christians. Now nine of my friends who weren't attending a church before are in *my* church. I love these people! I can't tell you what it means to me to have had a part in helping them move into faith."
- "I believe so strongly in the church and the power of God to heal people's lives through this community."
- "I've been praying for prisoners. We have a prison ministry in our church. Four of these people now have a relationship with Jesus. It has changed my life, too."
- "I love the feeling of working with the Spirit that I get when I pray for someone. Sometimes later there's an opportunity to share with them about God. These openings feel miraculous. And if that person comes to faith in Christ from that conversation, it's the most amazing feeling. You know you've helped God change someone's life forever. And the thing is, it's really just being open to God. You pray and wait and then the Spirit does the work."

So, what motivates you?

> What's at stake in evangelism is transformed lives, yours included!

DISCUSSION QUESTIONS _____

1. How is your individual prayer going? Spend the first 10 minutes of your time together sharing the highlights of your prayer time with each other. How have you seen God this week?

2. Did any Bible passage come to mind when you read this chapter? Does one occur to you now? Discuss how it connects with what

you have read. (If no passages come to mind, you might want to look at: John 3:16–17; John 20:30–31; Isaiah 45:22–23; and Isaiah 55:1–3.)

3. How do *you* feel when you hear the word *evangelism?*

4. What difference does being a Christian make in your life?

5. Why does it matter that other people become Christians? Use the "motivational pitcher" to talk about what motivates you to do evangelism, and what drains you.

At the beginning of each session:

A. Light a candle to remind us of Christ's presence;

B. Repeat aloud, together: "**We agree that we will hold everything shared in this group in complete confidence.**"

EXERCISE

Divide into clusters of three people. Try to be with the people you know the **least** well! The leader will keep time and signal the end of each time period with a bell or a gong. Sit comfortably in silence for two minutes. During the silence, ask God to remind you of a time when you were aware of God's presence. God might show you a conversion experience, or a feeling of the Christ Child's presence a healing, a miracle or something that happened this week in your prayer time.

The key is to ask God which story or memory to share with these other two people now. Ask God what *God* would like you to say. After the silence, each person has exactly four minutes to tell the story of how God was in his or her life. Don't interrupt or comment when the others are talking. Listen in silence and pray for the person as s/he speaks. Wrap up your story within half a minute of when the leader signals the end of your time.

You've just done faith sharing (evangelism). How was it?

Review pp.115–119 together now. Choose prayer partners. Start your prayer journal tomorrow.

---

[1] Annie Dillard, *Teaching a Stone to Talk* (Toronto, Ont.: HarperCollins, 1988), 40.

[2] Barbara Tuchman, *Practicing History* (New York: Alfred A Knopf, 1981), 134.

[3] Sword drills are Bible verse memorization tests and Bible search contests for kids. "Living in the Word" is an evangelical expression for steeping your life in scripture—living into it and living your life increasingly framed and guided by the teachings the Spirit puts in your heart from the Bible.

[4] One Midwestern pastor serves an old church with high numbers of transfers and adult baptisms. He is as theologically progressive as anyone with whom I spoke. He loves Jesus. This ex-missionary, ex-professor with a Ph.D. in world religions was enthusiastic and absolutely non-apologetic about offering Christianity as an option in Asia, and in the American city in which he now lives.

CHAPTER 2

Unbinding the Gospel—with Prayer

Three Stories of Victory

In an *Anne of Green Gables* book I read as a girl, Miss Cornelia, staunch pillar of the Presbyterian church, asked one of her friends about another woman's health. "Oh," Susan said, "I'm afraid she's going to have to rely on the Lord now." "Oh, no!" Miss Cornelia responded, "Surely it isn't as bad as all that?"[1]

You may suspect that Miss Cornelia was inquiring about the health of the mainline Church. "I'm afraid we're going to have to rely on the Lord now! Oh, no! Surely it isn't as bad as that?" Well, you know, it *is* as bad as that. People, families, churches, denominations and the aircraft carrier USS Nimitz don't make radical shifts in trajectory easily. Our denominations and many of our congregations have been on a downward pathway for decades. It would take a miracle to turn things around.

It will take a miracle to turn things around.

Isn't that what God has promised to do through us? Doesn't Jesus tell the disciples that they will do greater things than John the Baptist? (Lk. 7:28). Doesn't Jesus tell the disciples that after he left and the Spirit came, that they could do greater things than *he* could do? (Jn. 14:12). Doesn't Jesus tell the disciples that what they agreed on together in prayer God would do for them? (Mt. 18:19). We're the disciples. The decline of the mainline church is not merely serious. In Søren Kierkegaard's words, it is a "sickness unto death." We must not ignore this fact.

We must do the only realistic thing. We need to look the facts in the face, to pray that God lets us continue to love and honor God,

> It would take a miracle to turn things around.
>
> Isn't that what God has promised to do through us?

and to see the state of the churches with as much clarity as each one of us is able to bear. Then we can ask God to guide us, step by step, to do whatever things we're each supposed to be doing. If we really believe in crucifixion and resurrection, in a life of worshiping God and surrendering self, what real option do we have but to let God guide us through thought, study and open-spirited prayer?

A regional minister (bishop, synod executive) confessed at the beginning of a first long prayer retreat, "Well, you know I've been doing this ministry for 24 years now. We've strategized and prioritized and done mission statements that have kicked around the backs of closets. We've never prayed together except to say, 'God, bless this fight.' We've tried everything else; we might as well try prayer. What have we got to lose?"

How's it going under your own steam? Is it time to try to hand this church to God? Things change when people surrender time, choices and decisions to God. Are you ready to try it? Whatever you try won't be perfect. Yes, some congregations are too far in decline to turn around. Yes, many of us will have such needs for security that we will continue doing the same old things even though they haven't worked. Yes, not everyone will join in. Many dear, hardworking, faithful Christians—for one reason or another—will waste more energy and time, opportunities, life and money.

> We each touch the heart of the faith through our individual interactions with God. This relationship is nurtured in community. It is expressed through community. But at its center stands each of us, individually, being given glimpses of God's face.

But there really *is* a God. And we each need to decide if we're going to let God work through us and do miracles that accomplish amazing, unexpected things among us. There really *is* a God, and that God will nudge us into the most curious places—into conversations that are impossible to anticipate, in directions that we couldn't have thought out for ourselves.

After years of talking with pastors and laypeople in churches that are thriving, and in churches that are failing, I am clear that the only way to do ministry successfully, to lead a church or to live a life in today's United States is to pray deeply. We must hand ourselves over to God in clear-headed, accountable, non-naive prayer. We need to rely as much on God for pragmatic guidance as we can stand! Without God vividly in the mix, we drift, life declines.

What does trusting in the Lord look like? After all those statistics and hard facts in the introduction, it seems wrong to have some formulaic chapter on "How to Do Evangelism in Your Church." Instead, let's do what we might do if Jesus were here. Sit down and listen to some stories. Curl up on the sofa and hear what the Spirit might be saying through three stories of different churches. See what you think. The names are changed; denominations and locations are accurate.

Story One: What Do You *Mean,* "Sit and Pray"?

Benton Street Christian Church (Disciples of Christ) is a solid, healthy congregation. The staff is beloved. They have been together for 15 years. The church is administered efficiently and with grace. It has been growing smoothly and steadily for 15 years. People respect and like each other. The congregation is typically Midwestern, moderate to fairly progressive in theology, with deep biblical roots. The associate minister, Connie, has great relational gifts and a rich spiritual life. The church formed a new evangelism team a year and a half ago. I met them for lunch as they started. The four women's energy and excitement impressed me immediately. They kept asking me what to do. For once in my life, I didn't tell them. I felt they were up to a challenge, so instead I said, "Will you all trust me?"

> We work so *hard*, but the joy, the "first love," the "in love" feelings with God can fade to dusty duty, good works, more work.

"Sure, Martha Grace, anything you say."

"Would you spend three months praying together and not do anything else, not make any decisions for three whole months?"

"WHHHAAAAAATTTTTT?????"

"Yes," I murmured sadistically. "You three pray. Meet every week for at least an hour. Pray for the church, for the members, for discernment and for the people you don't even *know* that God would love to be able to bring to Benton Street. Pray that you'll be open. Pray for each other and what's going on in your lives. Pray that God will show you what you're to do and that God will nudge the right people to help you. But promise me that you won't make any decisions or do any "work" for three months. You can read a few books, but mainly pray, okay? What do you think?"

"Can Connie lead our meetings?" (In grief theory, this is known as "bargaining.")

"Why don't you pray about whether she should lead the meetings?"

"Oh. Hmmm. Okay."

So began an Agony and Ecstasy three months. The evangelism team prayed together frequently (**with** Connie present, **without** Connie leading). Every morning at 7:30, wherever they were, they prayed. They read books and searched the Internet. They went to board meetings every month and reported what they were doing. Everyone asked, "Ok, so what is your committee doing now?" They gave their report: "We're still praying. We're not allowed to make any decisions yet, but we are praying for you all and the church and the new people." This was no typical committee report, but the board laughed and loved it. The evangelism team received some gentle ribbing. Then they started getting prayer requests.

Exactly four months after our lunch, Connie told me that at the end of their three-month sentence, the team of three women had leapt out of the starting gate like Preakness winners. Now almost 50 people were helping with evangelism. I blurted,

"Wwwwwhhhhhaaaaatttttttt?????"

"Yea, they're welcoming people in worship and talking about the Spirit. Right after the worship service, we encourage visitors to pick up a small gift at our new welcome center. People bake bread, and "Loafers" deliver it to first-time visitors. We have other gifts for first-time visitors at a welcome center outside the sanctuary. There's a computer analyst keeping lists of visitors and we're praying for them. They've decided that we may be situated by God to have a ministry to the apartment complex near the church."

Later on, the evangelism team had 65 members, including intercessors and thank-you gift teams, designers of little feedback and prayer cards. A schizophrenic person visited one Sunday. A social worker pitched in to do follow-up. Visitors were increasing, return visitors were increasing, baptisms were increasing, baby dedications were increasing. I met with the team ten months into the experiment. They were thrilled. They were starting to get a little tired. I asked if they were praying as much. "Oh, oops. I guess we've sort of let that slip. It has been feeling dry and sort of like work. I guess we pick up the prayers again, right?" "Sounds like a plan," I agreed.

Connie wrote to me, "It was incredibly difficult for these four 'can-do' women to *wait* in prayer. All four of us have highly motivated, extremely organized, get-it-done personalities. A year and a half later, all four of us would say our prayer lives have been permanently impacted by this experiment. Two of us have moved into leadership in other areas of the church's ministry and are continuing to emphasize the importance and priority of prayer. The entire church is still being impacted by this willingness to risk praying first."

Exactly a year after our lunch, Benton Street held a board meeting at which the evangelism team presented their report. Instead of the traditional 6 or 7 infant dedications, they had 16, 15 of which were of children of new members or visitors. New members and visitors were involved in small groups. There were 80 new members. That was wonderful. But possibly as extraordinary was the fact that 65 long-term members of that church had a hand in praying and helping to

> We must do the only realistic thing. We need to look the facts in the face, to pray that God lets us see the state of the churches with as much clarity as each one of us is able to bear. Then we can ask God to guide us, step-by-step to do whatever things we're each supposed to be doing.

reach out to people they didn't know. Many of those lifelong Christians had experienced intercessory prayer and nudges from the Spirit for the first time in their lives. They felt it individually, they saw it together, and they heard those new voices in worship saying, "Yes, I accept Jesus Christ as my Lord and Savior." Benton Street members listened with lumps in their throats to the tight voices of parents vowing to raise their children in Christian homes. They are living in answered prayer; they are living *into* answered prayer.

Story Two: The Gift from Honduras

I placed hundreds of phone calls to pastors whose churches had the highest rates of adult baptisms in their denominations. These conversations transported me into the worlds of extraordinary congregations led by some wonderful men and women. One call I won't forget soon was with Don, the lead pastor of a 42-year-old Reformed Church in America (RCA) congregation in California. I explained about the evangelism study and told Don that his congregation was among a handful of mainline churches across the country that were doing lots of adult baptisms. I asked him to tell me what made the church tick, what motivated the members, what he believes, and how he leads.

So he started. He loves the church. Like most of the pastors who are doing lots of adult baptisms, he was surprised that they were doing relatively well (his church is in the top hundred in that pool of 30,000 mainline congregations). He talked for a solid 40 minutes about the church. He's been there for 12 years. He told me about worship decisions, what types of services they have (two contemporary and one traditional so they don't have to be too blended, which helps both their longer-term parishioners and the new people they're trying to reach). They've grown from 500 to about 960 adults in worship, not counting the 300 kids.

He told me about "life stage ministry" for the 20- and 30-year-olds and the gifted minister they have working with these younger folks. I heard about small groups, about Celebrate Recovery (a model for expressly Christian 12 step groups). Don told me about education classes they offer, ways they're working consciously to teach and integrate the new members they're attracting.

He was born and raised in the Reformed Church in America in the Midwest. He had his "fires lit" about evangelism as a young man—he's in his 40s now. The minute he started talking about evangelism and sharing the Gospel with new people, his voice gained energy. Then he told me more about what they're doing with the 25 to

> "For 24 years... we've strategized and prioritized and done mission statements that have kicked around the backs of closets. We've never prayed together except to say, 'God, bless this fight.' We've tried everything else: we might as well try prayer. What have we got to lose?"
>
> —*from a regional minister*

40 age group (contemporary praise music). He referred me to "this guy in San Jose who's doing amazing stuff with postmoderns—it's an RCA church plant specifically aimed at postmoderns and it's much edgier than anything we're doing." He talked about how important music is for younger people. He said they invite these younger adults to come forward and kneel for prayer and communion. These practices helps young adults worship in a way that feels real to them. Small groups foster intimacy, connection and peer relationships.

After at least 40 minutes, I asked a question. "You've been telling me amazing things about what God's doing in the church and in people's lives. You haven't mentioned prayer. Does prayer enter into your ministry in any special way?"

.......Silence......

"Oh, my gosh. Wow, don't let Beth, my wife, know I didn't say anything about prayer sooner." (He later told me it was okay to tell you this story. So did Beth.)

Prayer is the way to stay in love with God. Prayer is the way individuals, small groups and congregations grow and become vivid. It is a habit, a discipline, but not discipline with a clenched jaw.

"Oh, listen." *(Trust me, I was listening.)* "Prayer is a HUGE thing here. We have a prayer action team that's a group committed to fasting and prayer. They undergird every thing we do. You almost can't talk about it as a separate thing because the prayer is right there all the time. It has changed everything. Prayer makes openings, and we see possibilities and shifts and openings happening all the time. Now that I think about it, we really assume the Spirit's going to be leading."

"When did the praying start?" I asked him. "What does it look like? I take it Beth's very involved?"

"Six or seven years ago, Beth and I went to Community Church of Joy[2] for a week-long training event. It was great to be together and to get away for a new perspective. At the conference, you picked different sessions to attend. I went to the worship, administration and leadership sessions. Beth started going to sessions on prayer."

The prayer training affected Beth powerfully. On their return, she began to train a group of people to do intercession—to pray for others. In 2000, their classis (the Reformed Church version of a region, conference or synod) sponsored a joint workshop on prayer with the Moravian Church. A small group of Moravian Indian lay brothers from a tiny mountain town in Honduras were visiting. Beth and a couple of people from the church went. The brothers told about their ministry of intercession and fasting. Beth described the brothers to me in a later phone call. She was stunned by the men's simplicity, depth and integrity. During a later prayer retreat, the lay brothers taught 30 people from Beth and Don's congregation about prayer and fasting. Beth said that the most important thing the brothers taught them was to trust in the Spirit and to listen to God. Not talking. *Listening.*

"That was the beginning of another stage in the long journey," Don said. For two years, a changing group of 75 people participated in worship, praise, fasting and intercession for the first weekend of each month. "Now we have a group of four to six people praying for every single worship service. We have a group of intercessors for every minister in the church and a PIT team [Prayer and Intercession Team] for each ministry in the church."

Beth is a woman with a deep faith life. She is both wife and daughter of RCA ministers. She is a born teacher. As she explained prayer in the congregation, she had a clear grasp of ways people could begin to understand prayer and how they could move into deeper layers of experience. Her combination of deep sensitivity to the Spirit's promptings and her gift mix to teach, inspire and maintain relationships is clearly a major reason that prayer has taken such a deep hold in the congregation.

I asked what these nine years of learning and leading the prayer ministry had been like for her. Beth replied, "The best way I can describe it is as a journey. What I understand is changing; what we're led to do changes; we keep learning. I used to pray with lists: every Monday I prayed for the children's schools and their teachers and all the students. The next day I moved to my Tuesday list. Now I listen to God more and God gives me the people and the situations to pray for.

I asked her, "Can you articulate any differences the prayer makes in the congregation?"

"It's hard to say," she said. "Prayer is so subtle and so hidden. Sometimes it's hard to be part of the prayer ministry in the church because it never gets the big splash announcements in worship. We depend on word of mouth. Seeing results has a lag time. I'm starting to give workshops and teach in other churches. Often they're discouraged because maybe only three people will show up for a prayer event. I tell them that those must be the three God wants there that day. You have to let go of the idea that numbers matter or that it's visible results that count. That's very difficult for Americans in our culture to understand. It's hard not to have immediate results.

"But if we can leave the results of our prayer to God, if we can just praise God and listen to God rather than giving him a list of what we want, things do happen. On Friday this week, we're having a

Many of those lifelong Christians experienced intercessory prayer and nudges from the Spirit for the first time in their lives. They felt it individually, they saw it together, and they heard those new voices in worship saying, "Yes, I accept Jesus Christ as my Lord and Savior." Benton Street members listened with lumps in their throats to the tight voices of parents vowing to raise their children in Christian homes.

—Story 1

Halloween party for the children of the community. We're expecting about 2000 people from the community to visit our church. There will be "Prayer Walkers" moving through the crowd the entire time they are here. The Prayer Walkers are praying all the time, that specific children and parents will see Christ in something that happens, that some of the families will be moved to come to worship.

"We started using Prayer Walkers during our Vacation Bible School, praying that the children would learn, that this would change their lives. The number of children who made some kind of commitment to Christ has gone way up. We began having intercessors pray together [in a different room] during the entire four hours of our adult new members' class. There's a part in this first-level, introductory class where Don asks if anyone who has not become a Christian will make that decision and commitment. The number of those commitments has skyrocketed since we have been interceding for them."

How's it going on your own steam? Is it time to try to hand this church to God?

I asked Don if he could articulate how all of the prayer had changed things in the church. He said, "The spirit of the church is different. There are 'coincidences' that I know are answered prayer. We are more flexible. We have fewer disagreements. When we plan things, every once in a while someone will say, 'Wait a minute, what if we did this, instead?' Everyone will think about it for a minute, and many times we change direction. We can turn on a dime in this church. People are less attached to their own ideas and presuppositions. I haven't seen that happen, especially to this degree, anywhere else. You can't define it. You just get to know how different things are."

Story Three: Tuesday Mornings with the Guys

Andy is a thoughtful, gentle pastor with a quiet sense of humor. He has a humble spirit and has faithfully served First Presbyterian for over 20 years. He has done beautiful ministry, because the church hasn't shrunk. They have 125 people in worship (200 members). Their entire Midwestern county has only 4,500 people. The county has lost population every census since 1900, when they claimed 13,500 residents. The county has the same number of churches today as in 1900. This includes two small Methodist churches and an Assemblies of God new church start. Jobs disappear quietly. Many of the younger people and families have to move away to get better work. The town is not only shrinking, but the population is aging. So is the church. But, in a quiet voice, Andy talked about what it's like to serve these people and how hard they try.

About two years ago, a new Methodist minister came to town. The four pastors began to pray together every Tuesday morning for two hours. Andy said, "At first I thought, 'How in the *world* could I give two hours a week to pray with these guys?' Now I really miss it if we don't meet one week. It's really a support group as well as a prayer team. The competition between us is gone. That's a big thing, because we have four churches and only 1,700 people in the whole town. We've realized we're going after the people in town who aren't doing anything."

"How do you spend the two hours together?"

"Well, we talk a little bit about how each of us is doing and about where our churches are. We pray for each other, and for our churches, but then we're also praying for the people who don't attend any church. We have started praying for a revival."

"What's happening since you started praying? Has anything changed? Are you seeing any signs of a revival?"

"We're sort of shy people here. You have to be pretty brave to even ask people in church to break into small groups. And this thing with the pastors is not like any group I've ever been involved in. Things are happening, but it's hard to talk about. Pope John XXIII said to 'keep a window open for the Spirit.' That's one of the images I'm really working with—to keep a window open for the Spirit to do something. Things are changing. There's a real concern among the pastors for evangelism. That's different. The competition is gone. We're in this together. I think the Spirit's doing that.

"New people are coming to church —many of them are related to older, active members, but had never attended much. New things are happening. It's sort of a springtime season around here right now. Ministries are growing out of nowhere. People are starting to say, 'I think I need to do this,' and 'is that okay?' We just say, 'go to it, and blessings.'"

When one of the new members heard, "Go to it, and blessings," he went to it. Blessings followed. Greg is in construction. His new wife Sue is a lifelong member of the church. The Presbytery has a connection with a Catholic ministry to little villages in El Salvador. Greg and Sue were soon headed out on a "first-timers" mission. They loved the people. They loved helping. They caught on fire doing this kind of ministry!

Half of the children in the villages they visited die before they are five years old because of the poor quality of the drinking water. When they got home, Greg called a friend in the construction business who

> "Prayer is subtle and so hidden...You have to let go of the idea that numbers matter or that it's visible results that count. That's very difficult for Americans in our culture to understand...But if we can leave the results of our prayer to God, if we can just praise God and listen to God rather than giving him a list of what we want, things do happen."
> —*Beth, leader of a prayer ministry, Story 2*

had developed a drinking water purification system. They improved it to the point that the system operated with regular table salt, a car battery, and a hand crank.

Then Greg started to raise money because he thought it would be great to go back to El Salvador, taking three water pumps. Here's where a change came in. Andy, the pastor described it: "Greg started raising money, but it was different than any way we've ever done anything related to money. I'm pretty methodical. I've always done decision-making in the church through the session. The session is cautious about decisions. We're Presbyterians. We do things decently and in order!"

Greg didn't know a lot about either Presbyterians *or* their decent order. He stood up in worship and asked if people wanted to help with the water ministry. He and Sue sold bottles of water and said, "You'd pay $2.50 for this water at the ball game. How much would you pay for it if you didn't *have* any water?" They raised $4,500. The session dedicated $3,000 to the project. It was an accountable ministry with long-term ties to the presbytery. It wasn't a fly-by-night scheme. But a lightness entered into the church's traditional, responsible, dutiful ministry. People were having fun. Entire villages now have clean water.

Andy says they have introduced a few bits of new music in worship. Some of the older folks say, "Well, it's been okay so far, but you know if you take this to its logical conclusion, it could really get out of hand!"

Greg just got back from Africa, where he helped assemble ten prefabricated buildings for congregations that didn't have buildings yet. He and Sue are heading to Mexico at Christmas. "Everybody just watches them go, helps and cheers them on. And we're encouraged. Other people are doing new things, too." Andy tried to describe this new life in an old congregation with its veteran ministry. "Stuff just happens that you've been trying so hard to get going for *years*. All of a sudden something is blooming. You didn't even plant it and it's unfolding like a rose."

Windows Open for the Spirit

I don't want to tame these stories by analyzing them. I will make a few observations about prayer in alive and inspired congregations. Remember, we each touch into the heart of the faith through our individual interactions with God. This relationship is nurtured in

> Prayer is more about receiving from God than it is about asking God for things or working hard at intercession. Prayer involves effort, habit, and focus; but it results in lightness and energy and excitement.

community. It is expressed through community. But at its center stands each of us, individually, being given glimpses of God's face.

Many pastors and church leaders said essentially the same thing when I asked them if they had one piece of advice for people who want to do evangelism: "Tell them that you can't give what you don't have." "So much that can happen in the church is led or stopped by how healthy my relationship with Christ is." "It's consistent openness to God that really matters." The heart of faith sharing is one person giving another a vision of what it's like to be in love with God.

Remember the Spirit's word to the church at Ephesus? "I know your works, your toil and your patient endurance…I also know that you are enduring patiently and bearing up for the sake of my name and that you have not grown weary. But I have this against you, that you have abandoned the love you had at first" (Rev. 2:2–4). We work so **hard**, but the joy, the "first love," the "in love" feelings with God fade to dusty duty, good works, more work.

Prayer is the way to stay in love with God. Prayer is the way individuals, small groups and congregations grow and become vivid. It is a habit, a discipline, but not discipline with a clenched jaw. Prayer is more about receiving from God than it is about asking God for things or working hard at intercession. As you may have felt in these stories, prayer involves effort, habit and focus; but it results in lightness and energy and excitement.

My life has been characterized by hard work and fairly grueling discipline. I'm trying (really hard) to add a bit more lightness. This spring, I started voice lessons with a great teacher, Kate. I'm having fun! Last week I was gutting my way through a beautiful old Italian song and Kate said, "It's charming, but do you need to sound like a vacuum cleaner at the end of phrases?" I told her I thought I probably **did** need to suck air in like a vacuum because otherwise I would asphyxiate and crumple in a heap right there on her floor. "Look," she intoned majestically, "if you'll open up your ribs, the air just falls in."

That's what prayer does. If we will open our time to scripture, prayer, adoring God and listening to God, the inspiration of the Spirit just falls in. If we pray, we won't have to suck in inspiration like a shop vac. The whispers of the Spirit will nudge around the edges of our minds and surface in subtle ways. If we will open our ribs in prayer, inspiration will fall in. Many of our early Protestant forebears called this a "prepared heart." If we study scripture, pray

"Pope John XXIII said to 'keep a window open for the Spirit.' That's one of the images I'm really working with—to keep a window open for the Spirit to do something. Things are changing. There's a real concern among the pastors for evangelism. That's different. The competition is gone. We're in this together. I think the Spirit's doing that."

—*Pastor, Story 3*

and prepare ourselves to be used, God will direct us, lead us, use us for things God wants to do. It's as simple as that. The people in the stories in this chapter have discovered these small-step truths. Christ stands at the door knocking. Open your heart and Christ will enter in. We have the choice.

About Prayer

If you feel called to begin prayer like the people in this chapter, here are a few ideas and suggestions for you and your church:

1. A prayer life has two aspects—individual prayer and prayer with other people. These facets of prayer are inseparable. Don't try to go it alone. Don't freeload on the efforts of the rest of your prayer group. We must learn both to be alone with God and to pray in agreement with others. Try a daily prayer time. Spend time with God by yourself. Read scripture. Journal or pray for others. Sit silently and listen to God. Then pray with others. Pray alone. Pray with others. Both are crucial aspects of the rhythm of prayer.

2. Trusting God for guidance is counter-intuitive. It is particularly tough for self-reliant Americans. American culture has rarely held up surrender and yieldedness, the heart of a spiritual life, as heroic values. (Remember the thunderous prayer George C. Scott made as Patton after the 5th Army was taken away from him? "An entire *world* at war and me left out of it? This will not be *permitted* to happen! I will be allowed to *fulfill* my destiny. His will be done.")[3] All right, most of us aren't Patton; but we do tend to set out to pray and hand Christ our lives to be used, then yank the control back. ("Gosh, God, thanks for the tip! That was *amazing*! Okay, so, I can take it from here.") Be aware of the tendency to trust God, then to snatch the reins from the Spirit's fingers.

3. Prayer is a lifelong practice. Praying feels miraculous at first. If we can get past the "I'll take it from here" impulses and get to the point where solitary prayer and praying with others become a normal part of our lives, the rhythms of trust in God and God's providence become as natural as driving a car. Remember that Don, the California pastor, didn't think to mention prayer in a congregation steeped in intercession? When I asked him after 40 minutes of conversation whether they prayed in any specific way, he was stunned. I suspect this is because prayer has become so ingrained a part of life that in one way it didn't feel like an activity they *do*. He didn't mention prayer. He didn't mention tooth brushing. He never told me that people in their church exhale.

"New things are happening. Ministries are growing out of nowhere. People are starting to say, 'I think I need to do this,' and, 'Is that okay?' We just say, 'Go to it, and blessings.'"

—*Pastor, Story 3*

4. We need someone to help us learn prayer. Although our Protestant heritage is rich in prayer resources, the memory and training have thinned and faded in the last century. Our images of people who pray are more weighted toward cartoons of pious little people (who in reality may be spiritual heavyweights) than toward images of Martin Luther King praying before the Mall speech. Prayer isn't a sweet, nice, safe, naive little activity to do in your flowery hat. It is crash helmet action for people who flip kayaks in raging spring rivers. If you want to begin to pray seriously, please find a guide who knows the spiritual currents before your kayak sideswipes boulders under the water's surface. Chapter 6 offers more discussion of the realities of a congregation's prayer life.

Ask God to bring someone into your life or church who has prayed seriously for years. People like Beth (Story 2, *A Gift from Honduras*) teach prayer. I have heard mainline people who now pray in earnest mention beginning to pray with a Benedictine sister spiritual director, an Orthodox Church in America theology professor, a Southern Baptist evangelical friend, a Catholic priest from Botswana, an American Baptist pastor who's also a Jungian analyst, or a new neighbor who goes to the Vineyard Church. Please get help from people from different backgrounds.

You do not need to subscribe wholeheartedly to someone's theology to ask them to pray with you and for your ministry. If you get advice that feels strange, remember that learning about new areas of the faith is like eating fish. Eat what is good and spit out the bones. Ask God to show you the parts you need, and don't worry about the rest of it.

5. We need discernment and accountability. Can things get out of control when churches begin to pray? How can you tell an idea is from God and not spun out of your own fevered imagination? These are issues of spiritual maturity.

Look at the synergy between joy, excitement and accountability in the story of the Presbyterian church in the dwindling Midwestern town (*Tuesday Mornings with the Guys*). People were jazzed up with inspiration and hot ideas, but they talked them over with the church. The session (council) didn't stop the momentum, but after thoughtful discernment, joined in supporting a long-term Presbytery ministry. A life steeped in prayer is exciting and filled with change. It is not a life of froth or unconscious acting out. We need practice, accountability to a group of Christians, and wise counselors to help us discern which ideas are nudges from God and how they should be acted upon.

> Prayer isn't some sweet, nice, safe, naive little activity to do in your flowery hat. It is crash helmet action for people who flip kayaks in raging spring rivers. If you want to begin to pray seriously, please find a guide who knows the spiritual currents before your kayak sideswipes boulders under the water's surface.

Think about scriptures like Galatians 2:2, in which Paul felt strongly about what he was to do, but went to Jerusalem to consult with the leaders of the Jerusalem church to make certain that they were in agreement.[4] Be open to the Spirit. Remember you don't have all the answers. You need the wisdom of others to navigate the currents. Be open to the Spirit. Don't be naive.

Unbinding the Gospel
Matthew 18:15–20

In Matthew 18, Jesus tells the disciples, "Whatever you bind on earth will be bound in heaven, and whatever you loose on earth will be loosed in heaven" (Mt. 18:18). *We* are also given the power to untie or unbind things. As disciples of Christ, we have the power to affect great things. In the scripture, Jesus then says, "If two of you agree on earth about anything you ask, it will be done for you by my Father in heaven" (Mt. 18:19).

My friend Don Schutt is certain Jesus could make this promise because it's so hard to get two or three people to agree about ***anything***! Don says, more seriously, that this mysterious passage means that if we try to discern the deep realities of a situation so that we can pray about it together, in sync with God's will, that it enables God to use our prayer to accomplish God's desires. If we will think about a situation, pray to understand it, talk together and pray in the agreement of the understanding the Spirit has given us, our prayer will be Christ's prayer. This is the kind of spiritual power the churches in the three stories in this chapter have experienced.

Many of the dear churches we love are inflexible. Many churches are tied into knots of self-involvement or old habit. Most of us are fairly knotted up as people. We're anxious, worried, stewing, angry or afraid. The Gospel is about freedom in Christ. Think of all the strands that tie us up—death, sin, fear, anger, addictions, nasty gossiping, fussy tediousness, age-old resentments, self-involvement! The Gospel, the Good News, is about freedom in Christ. It is about knots being untied, ropes loosened, ties unbound.

Every one of us is too narrow in our understanding. We don't want upsets in our lives, or changes in our habits, or threats to our opinions. Shifting from Shredded Wheat™ to oatmeal exhausts me on a bad day! Telling God it's okay to change an institution I lean into for my stability (like my church) is really scary. But we need to do it. Many churches are slowing down because they are running on

Prayer

1. A prayer life has two parts—individual prayer and prayer with others.
2. Trusting God for guidance is counter-intuitive.
3. Prayer is a lifelong practice.
4. We need someone to help us learn prayer.
5. We need discernment and accountability.

our human steam. I'm afraid we're going to have to rely on the Lord now. ("Oh, no! Surely it isn't as bad as all that?")

Do you dare risk agreeing with some others in your church to pray together and see what God can do? Do you dare **not** risk it?

DISCUSSION QUESTIONS _____

1. How is your individual prayer going? Spend the first 10 minutes of your time together sharing the highlights of your prayer time with each other. How have you seen God this week?

2. What Bible passages came to mind when you read this chapter, or occur to you now? Discuss how they connect with what you have read. (If you don't think of any passages, you might want to look at: Matthew 18:18–20; Mark 4:1–9; Galatians 2:1–2; Revelation 2:1–7.)

3. Which of these stories of prayer is most exciting or attractive to you? Do they seem real? Possible? Impossible in your context? Why? Did anything stir up resistance in you? Repel you?

4. What experience with prayer or intercession have you had? How is your experience similar to these stories? How do you think your congregation might react to prayer of this type? Who do you know who might be interested in praying like this? Are you one of them?

5. What prevents you from risking to agree with some others in your church to pray together and see what God can do? Do you dare *not* risk it?

At the beginning of each session:

A. Light a candle to remind us of Christ's presence;

B. Repeat aloud, together: "**We agree that we will hold everything shared in this group in complete confidence.**"

EXERCISE _____

Are you willing to pray for two other people each day for the next week? If so, divide into small groups of three. (Choose two other people you know least well. Try to sit with different people than last week. The leader will keep time again.)   First, sit in silent prayer for three minutes. As you breathe deeply and get quiet inside, ask God to let you know one thing you will ask your friends to pray about for you. It may be forgiveness, strength to go through each day without satisfying your addiction, for healing, for a healing of anger, for boundaries, for a growth in patience or love, or for discernment.

There's only one rule: the prayer must be for *you*— not your mother-in-law, your child, or people at work. Ask God what *you* need prayer for. After the silence, tell the others how they can focus their prayer for you in one short, timed minute. As soon as you have all shared your prayer requests, pray for each other.

Will you risk a six-month experiment in your church? Will you open every meeting in the church for six months this way, by praying for each other? Spend the first 10 minutes of every meeting praying for each other for real, in these little groups of three. Are you brave enough? It's just a six-month trial at the beginning of every single board meeting, elders' meeting, women's and men's and youth meeting, grass-mowing-gutter-cleaning-out group meeting. Pray about whether you're supposed to risk it.

If You Want to Go Further

If this chapter has been of interest to you and you'd like to go further with learning about prayer, you might want to look at Joe Driskill's *Protestant Spiritual Exercises* (Morehouse), Richard Foster's *Prayer: Finding the Heart's True Home* (HarperSanFancisco), or use the prayer journals in the other *Unbinding* books.

A life steeped in prayer is exciting and filled with change. It is not a life of froth or unconscious acting out. We need practice, accountability to a group of Christians, and wise counselors to help us discern which ideas are nudges from God and how they should be acted upon.

---

[1]Lucy M. Montgomery, *Anne's House of Dreams* (New York: Grosset and Dunlap, 1917).

[2]A huge, 30-year-old Lutheran (ELCA) church just north of Phoenix. They are on the high adult baptism list. They also host educational events that have shaped the ministries of quite a few of the pastors and lay leaders with whom we spoke during this study. See the bibliography at www.GraceNet.info for books by their pastor Walt Kallestad. Visit Community Church of Joy's Web site at www.joyonline.org.

[3]*Patton,* 20th Century Fox, 1970.

[4]"I went up [to Jerusalem] in response to a revelation. Then I laid before [the leaders of the church]…the gospel that I proclaim among the Gentiles, in order to make sure that I was not running, or had not run, in vain" (Gal. 2:2).

CHAPTER 3

Real Life

By the end of college, my friends and I sounded like accomplished jazz musicians when we set off into our polished riffs on the theme, "It's time to get out of this ivory tower and get on to Real Life." Flies on the wall must have giggled a couple of years later to see us spiffed up as if in our mommies' dresses, lipstick and high heels. There we were in crisp suits (with stapled hems and paper clip buttons), carrying our unscarred briefcases, blackboard chalk, shiny stethoscopes and efficient stacks of files with desperate casualness. Real jobs, real paychecks—this is *great*!

The real deadlines, real car payments, real mortgages, real 2 a.m. feedings came next. Then the real car pool schedules, real shopping lists, real tax returns, real office politics, real layoffs, real marriage problems, real affairs began to exert deadly gravity.

At our tenth reunion we ditched the suits, slung on jeans and hiking boots, and stayed up talking till 4 a.m. to find out what was really going on in each other's lives. The talking, the reconnections, reimmersed us in the reality of being with people who would love us no matter what. We remembered what it was like to be with the ones who knew every secret, every screw-up, every foible in the past—the ones who cared. After spilling out everything, one woman looked up through tear-filled eyes and said, "Oh, my gosh, it's such a relief to get back with you guys—I've needed so badly to be able to be *real*."

That's what being a Christian ought to feel like.

Being a Christian should be the most real *real* there is. It should feel like coming home to a place where you are exposed to so many new ideas you can't integrate them quickly enough; of cheering for

A Christian is a powerful individual on a powerful team. It's a life with no posturing, no pretending. That's the *real* real life!

43

your team, surrounded by your friends; of beginning to take risks and make adult choices alone for the first time in your life; of being able to say anything that pops into your mind because you're hanging out with the people you can trust with your life, of going back each September and meeting the new kids and showing them the ropes. That's what being a Christian ought to feel like, a powerful individual on a powerful team: a life with no posturing, no pretending. That's the *real* real life!

At its best, Christian life has two aspects that are inseparable. It must be real (honest, transparent), and it must be relational (be lived in relationships that are real/honest/transparent). Most churches don't come close because they're too involved in the quasi-real lives of briefcases, car pools, and covering your back from office politics. But God can create, redeem and sustain churches that are real.

A Trinity of Real Life

This real Christian life is a bit like the Trinity that God is. The Trinity is an enormous mystery. God is one God, indivisible, and at the same time three: Father, Son and Holy Spirit; or, as some say, Creator, Redeemer and Sustainer. The Trinity is a concept worked out in the earliest days of the church. It is embodied in our creeds. It is hard to understand. Somehow the impossibility of the idea of One and Three flips our minds into a little understanding of something very important. A vivid relationship lives in God's heart.

Think about the Trinity, God as One and Three, at the same time you consider another primary understanding of Christianity. We, as individuals, are made in God's image. So the doctrine of the Trinity must say something about who we can be as people and how Christ's Church (Christ's body) can be. The doctrine of the Trinity, the idea that God is made up of relationships, shows us something important about the nature of people and church.

I have seen many powerful, faithful churches during this study. The ones that have seemed most "real" have felt creative and complex. They support members' actions, growth and initiatives, while leaving space for each individual. No matter how clear they are about a few essentials, the best of these churches don't force rigid conformity on less crucial issues.

The great churches aren't mushily, sentimentally, smotheringly "caring." They aren't "damn the torpedoes, full speed ahead." They aren't all Venus; they aren't all Mars. They're messy. They allow intuition, action and spontaneity, while providing teaching, support,

Great churches aren't mushily, sentimentally, smotheringly "caring." They aren't "damn the torpedoes, full speed ahead." They aren't all Venus; they aren't all Mars. They're messy. They allow intuition, action and spontaneity while providing teaching, support, correction and accountability. They feel alive. They're in touch with joy. God is all over them. The Spirit is palpable.

correction and accountability. They feel alive and almost always are in touch with joy. These churches are real. God is all over them. The Spirit is palpable.

I want to use the Trinity that is God as a metaphor for the way these churches live, operate and do evangelism. These churches all have three sets of relationships that are distinct yet which constantly interact and affect each other. These three sets of relationships are:

1. with God,
2. between church members and
3. with people outside church.

A Trinity of Relationships

Relationships with God

Relationships with People Outside the Church

Relationships between Church Members

If we pastors don't talk about our lives with God, if we don't have substantial prayer lives, it is not likely that members of our churches will develop much of a spiritual life, either. If members are not afire with love for God, it is inconceivable that they will do much to share their faith. Why would we *think* evangelism would happen?

God works powerfully through these three sets of relationships in healthy churches. These great churches, large and small, have a spider-web wholeness about them. Touch one area of the web, and ripples shimmer across its entire surface. As individual relationships with God grow, people are able to be more real with each other within the church. As relationships within the church get richer, members of the church somehow know how to be better friends at work, in the neighborhood, coaching Little League. But if relationships with people outside the church—with neighbors, friends and far away family—begin to deteriorate, prayer time may falter. Then, the congregation may edge into isolation. Everything affects everything!

Positively or negatively, these sets of relationships affect each other. If one area grows and gets healthier, the other areas will change. Congregational leaders must pay attention to all three areas if the church is to thrive and do healthy ministry/evangelism. A congregation that is out of balance, with strength in only one or two areas, is merely limping along. Let's try to get a healthier balance by examining each of these three areas.

Individuals' Relationships with God

We had a great idea in the Mainline Evangelism Project. We asked almost all 1000 people interviewed, and over 400 people who filled in written surveys, for the best piece of advice they could give someone who is trying to help people become Christians. One of the most frequent answers advised that our relationships with God are the foundation stone of who we are as Christians. Pastors often say, "As pastor, I can't teach what I don't know." Leaders of evangelism teams talk about praying for others and keeping in touch with God themselves. Doesn't it make sense that if doing evangelism is about helping others connect with God's love, then the more connected we are with God ourselves, the better we'll be able to do our parts?

Let's hear directly from some of the people whose churches are doing wonderful evangelism with unchurched people. Here are exact responses to the question: "What one sentence of advice would you give to someone in your position who is trying to reach unchurched people?"

Churches where people snap, snipe, pull power plays over the budget, then go home to fried preacher for Sunday supper don't do good evangelism over the long haul!

Advice from senior pastors:

- "Be a living example, pray."
- "Some of the most important things I have been able to teach are the things God just taught me. I'll go through some big struggle with God who will teach me something in my own life. Two days later one of my elders will call me to have lunch and what I just learned will be *exactly* what she needed to hear. I can't see it as coincidental after all these years. It's a God rhythm."
- "You can't give what you don't got—your relationship with God must be hot!"

Advice from laypeople highly involved in evangelism:

- "Keep in prayer for opportunities to witness about your faith, or answer questions someone has."
- "First pray, then accept training and discipline and then practice with more prayer!"
- "Demonstrate the power of Jesus by showing kindness, love, compassion, understanding, humility. Be honest and sincere and show them the love of God within you."

Advice from a new Christian:

- "[Our UCC church] is growing very rapidly due to the pastor and his closeness to God that he shares with all of us."

Having just listed all these quotes, I feel some discomfort. Those of you in churches with a healthy "relationship with God" emphasis will read the advice to attend to your spiritual life and will be nodding along, thinking, "Well, of *course*." But most of us are in mainline churches with a very light emphasis on relationship with God. And if we don't know what having a healthy spiritual life looks or smells or feels like, if we're good members of our churches, if we're faithful pastors who are working hard, we think we understand. We'll read this advice, nod, and think, "Well, of *course*." But we won't get it.

Churches that emphasize a growing relationship with God for its members, board and pastors are different than "normal" churches. I don't want to sound critical, but visiting one of these vibrant churches makes attending many of our mainline congregations feel like going to a Lions Club meeting—a good thing, certainly, but not the real thing.

Do you remember the three stories in chapter 2 about congregations that started praying? In two of them, the prayer (and the experiences that the Spirit led the people into) felt very new to most of the people involved. That is a typical mainline response to beginning to pray. We have not had much training. I loved my seminary. I will always be grateful for the people and for what I learned during my years there. But when I attended, in the late 1980s, no prayer class was offered. Except for a bit in hospital chaplaincy training, the only discussion or training in prayer I had in my three-year seminary studies was a half an hour during the worship class on how to compose and lead the pastoral prayer in the Sunday worship service.

I had a fairly rich spiritual life personally, because I grew up outside the church and became a Christian in Spain as a college student. Brilliant evangelical college kids nurtured me through my first year as a Christian, so I had a year of learning fasting and prayer, of devouring devotional Bible reading and theology, and of intense Bible study and prayer for each other in a small group. After my seminary training, as a 35-year-old, self-confident ex-lawyer, I began serving my first congregation. I made my first hospital call on a founding member of the church who died the next day. I did not know how to pray with her, or with her family. I thought it might offend them, or be invasive. I knew people expected a chaplain to pray in the ICU. I knew how evangelicals prayed, but that had somehow been dismantled in me and nothing rebuilt in its place. So I listened and empathized, counseled and left. I think of that day now and cringe. I failed that woman and her family.

The more each of us looks to Christ and asks for forgiveness for our gaffs, foibles and mess-ups, the more likely we are to hear other people's ideas, to forgive and to get along. The more the Spirit is leading, the more energy is freed to go into gear. We will experience fewer power struggles and more joy.

If faith and church have changed your life, you'll want others to understand that there is no sin, no resentment, no bitterness, no wound, no fear, no illness, no loneliness that Christ cannot forgive, dissolve, heal, cure, fill. You'll want everyone to know that the God of infinity is there to lead them by the hand into forever. Nothing is more real than this good news.

I wish I could look back on that hospital visit as the normal fumbling of an inexperienced pastor. It *was* that, but I think my discomfort, my ignorance, revealed a blank spot in the mainline experience. I think this blank spot, this gap, is helping cause the declines in our churches you read about at the beginning of chapter 3. I have spent the last ten years working with hundreds of mainline pastors. Many of them know that they "aren't evangelical," (meaning "not biblical literalists"), but there's nothing rebuilt in that spot. What do we believe *positively*?

Many, many mainline pastors do not have a regular personal prayer life. Many are surprised by an offer to close a phone conversation with prayer. I have asked many pastors as we end a phone call, "Is there any specific way I can focus my prayer for you?" A typical response is, "Wow, I never had anyone ask me that. Let me think a minute." The response is usually a heartfelt request.

We in the mainline, even pastors, can be shy people when it comes to our faith. If we pastors don't talk about our lives with God, if we don't have a substantial prayer life, it is not likely that the members of our churches will be developing much of a spiritual life, either. If members are not afire with love for God, from a vivid sense of what God is doing every day, it is inconceivable that they will do much to share their faith with others. *Why* would we think evangelism would happen?

The good news is that mainline pastors and mainline church members can learn to pray and can develop spiritual disciplines. It's like getting into the habit of an exercise program. Of *course* it would have been easier if you'd been exercising since your high school track star days. But do something for 21 days, and it becomes a habit! Try asking God to give you a subtle nudge (or a smack upside the head) within the next couple of days with an opportunity to do something to make God more real and personal in your life.

More good news is that there are several movements within the mainline churches that are helping reignite interest in the spiritual disciplines. We can learn from Christians from all backgrounds—evangelical, charismatic, catholic, orthodox. Be brave. Make some phone calls! Go to lunch. Ask questions. Ask Christ.

If you and your congregation do not have a primary focus on having a relationship with God, please ask the Spirit to help you change that. Everything depends on it.

Relationships within the Church

The second part of the "Relationships' Trinity" is the relationships within the church. Congregations that are doing great faith teaching/ faith sharing over the long haul are healthy from the inside out. If individuals are devoted to staying alive in Christ and have a spiritual life that is sustained over time, if the congregation puts a long-term focus on helping people be in primary contact with God, then healthy relationships have a much better chance of developing. Churches where people snap, snipe, pull power plays over the budget, then go home to fried preacher for Sunday supper don't do good evangelism for the long haul![1]

Members of growing churches usually love going to church! Why would this surprise us? If you love your church, if being part of it is adding good things to your life, if you're learning, if your kids love youth group, you probably think your friends would get something out of church, too!

More hardworking, smart, kind Christians than I can count have said to me, "Well, I just can't invite people to our church. Our friends are here. We've been here forever, so we're committed; but I just don't want other people to have to get into it." You and other people in your church reading this book together may feel this way yourselves. Could you be brave enough to say it out loud?

I asked an elder and former board chair who had sat in the front row of the choir of her church every Sunday for 30 years, "Why do you go to church? What do you get out of it?" Her husband of 35 years had just died slowly and painfully. Horror stories pocked her memories of her marriage and raising the children. She answered, "Church has always meant a lot to me because I knew that if things got really bad, I could tell someone about it." I asked if she ever *had* talked with anyone about anything really bad. "No, but I always knew that I *could* have."

That is not the type of church that warms people's hearts and draws them to Christ's love by way of their deepest yearnings. Yet when people were asked to describe this congregation, the two most frequent responses were that it was "friendly" and "it's like family here." Here's the question: Do you tell people in your church what's really going on in your life? (Not *could* you, but *do* you?)

Churches with healthy relationships don't experience a lot of ego-wrangling. People in these churches (individually, in small groups

THE TEST:

Do you tell people in your church what's really going on in your life? (Not *could* you, but *do* you?)

and all together in worship) are trying to yield their lives to Christ to be shaped and used. The more each one of us looks to Christ each day and asks for forgiveness for our gaffs, foibles and mess-ups, the more likely we are to be able to hear other people's ideas, to forgive and to get along. The more each of us is looking to Christ every day, the more likely we will be to share what's really going on in our lives, to help each other, and to pray for each other.

The more the Spirit is leading each person and each group, the more conflict recedes. The more the Spirit is leading, the more creativity, energy, and outward focus are freed to go into gear. People in love with God and serving each other live with joy. Life is less power struggle, and more fun.

So what does an alive, relationally healthy church look like? Decades ago, the United States Supreme Court was asked to consider a case involving obscenity laws. Many people wanted the court to define obscenity for the whole country. The court declared that a definition wouldn't work because communities are different. (For example, it's probable that more people in rural Minnesota would think a film or an advertisement obscene than the same number of people in certain sections of San Francisco or New Orleans.) Justice Potter Stewart wrote in a concurring opinion that he wasn't going to attempt to define obscenity, "but I know it when I see it."[2]

It's like that with a great church. People ask me to define them. I wouldn't **attempt** to find some ultimate definition of a church with healthy internal relationships. It can look totally different, depending on whether it's in piney Louisiana or in the Bronx. One thing is certain, though: people know it when they see it. Visitors can feel it when they step across that threshold.

Listen to some descriptions from people talking about healthy, loving churches:

from new Christians:

■ "I am very blessed to be a member of First Congregational Church. It is rich in its 100-plus–year history and it is rich in love for family and community, and for mission. The church members always have a warmth that would make any new visitor feel welcome and right at home. That was one of the many reasons that I felt so good about becoming a member of this church and this family."

■ "The members here support each other."

■ "My church is a very loving, supportive, and caring church. My church always makes sure newcomers feel welcomed. I felt so

---

Healthy Relationships in Churches

1. People are real. They are honest. They share their lives with each other in significant ways rather than putting on a "perfection show."

2. People see each other for who they are, and show respect by telling the truth lovingly.

3. Relationships are not sentimental. People acknowledge their own frailties and sinfulness. They may have disagreements, but they find ways of resolving them without undue conflict or long resentments.

4. Visitors can feel it when they walk in the door!

loved and that I mattered to everyone when my children and I first attended. My pastor is such an amazing man. His love for Jesus shines all over his face. He is a very important part of my children and I choosing to become members here. When you walk into our church, you can feel the Holy Spirit with the worship and love all around you. It feels like Jesus is with us clapping and singing. I know He is very pleased how much He is loved."

from a new member

■ "With regard to my church: it is very real, very relevant, very comfortable for everyone to be who they are and where they are in their spiritual journey. There is an abundance of love and support and caring, which radiates outward from the pastors through everyone in their wake. Anyone in proximity to these guys gets a real 'Jesus Glow.' How cool is that?"

Evangelistic churches live out real life, real relationships—with God and with each other. And, contrary to what happens in other places, what happens in church doesn't *stay* in church. Lives are transformed in the congregation. Those changes move out into everyone's lives and all their other relationships. The power of the loving church can't stop at the door, or it will turn inward and fade. Let's take a look at the third part of this trinity of relationships.

> Church is an igniter of faith that affects your whole life. Members of great congregations think of spiritual growth; surrender of self; healing of bodies, addictions, marriages, wounded souls; and serving others when they hear the word church.

Real Relationships Christians Carry into the Rest of Their Lives

Vibrant congregations contain people who are attending to spiritual disciplines and alive in Christ. Live congregations, where relationships within the church are nurtured and where the congregation tries to work together in the Spirit, change people's lives. Church is no longer a "place to go." It isn't just for Sunday morning. It isn't the ticket you punch to get new clients and make useful contacts. Church isn't the place you go weekly for "a little encouragement to get you through the rest of the week." Church is an igniter of faith, an instigator of growth that affects your whole life. Thinking extraordinary new ideas about surrender of self, healing of bodies, addictions, marriages, wounded souls, and serving others—these thoughts come to mind when members of great congregations hear the word "church."[3]

Church merges with real life. If faith and church have changed your life, you'll want to share that discovery with your friends. You want everyone to know that Christ lives. You want everyone to know that God loves us extravagantly. You want everyone to know that God will overwhelm their souls with grace and wash away sins. You want everyone to understand to the soles of their feet that there is no sin, no resentment, no bitterness, no wound, no fear, no illness, no loneliness that Christ cannot forgive, dissolve, heal, cure, fill. You want everyone to know that God, the Great I Am, the God who says, "before Abraham *was*, I *AM*," the God of infinity is there to lead them by the hand into forever, into an eternity of powerful love. Nothing is more beautiful than this good news.

Understanding these things unbinds the Gospel. Understanding these things frees captives, including us. Understanding these things gives people the ability to choose real freedom. Once we understand this, the only question is how to help people hear it clearly. Our questions shift from, "Why would I do *evangelism*?" to, "Oh, Lord, *how* can I help people see your face? Who do you want me to pray for? Show me today, lead me to the ones you can reach through me. Please show us how our church can serve you, how we can better organize ourselves to help you. Let us be a part of what you want to do next."

Hundreds of new and old Christians, members and pastors of great congregations, have told us of their desire to share their faith. One person responded to the question, "What advice would you give to someone like you who is trying to reach unchurched people?" by writing, "Be loving and let God set the opportunity to tell them about Jesus. It might be of interest to know that I came to the Lord after I was married at age 23 through my neighbor who had been a Christian for one day. She had no knowledge or strategy."

The new Christian wants to hand on the excitement within 24 hours. This Gospel can't be contained! Is it just new Christians who are excited about sharing faith? Not on your life. A 60-year-old, lifelong Christian described a new type of Bible study for teenagers: "It was amazing! This new way of working with the kids entranced them. I couldn't get them out the door (not that I was trying too hard)! Computerized Bible scavenger hunt put together with acting, and kids were moved to prayer and commitment. I can never anticipate what God is going to do next or how people will respond. Sharing Him is the adventure of my life."

A female pastor from the East Coast went to a Midwestern Presbyterian congregation as an interim minister, but is going to be able to stay as the permanent pastor. She's a happy woman and a smart one. She loves the congregation and kept saying, "We're having so much *fun* here. These people are wonderful." In two short years,

Once you have a rich faith life and a healthy church, your questions shift from, "Why would I do *evangelism*?" to, "Oh, Lord, *how* can I help people see your face? Show me today, lead me to the ones you can reach through me. Let me be part of what you want to do next."

she has helped begin Bible studies, create a neighborhood food pantry, send kids on mission trips, establish Great Banquet participation (the Presbyterian Cursillo/Walk to Emmaus movement), and perform six or eight adult baptisms a year. She loves reaching out to people. The congregation is loving it, too.

First Reformed Church is seeing an influx of Hispanic migrant workers into their traditional city. Demographics are changing dramatically. The reserved, Dutch descendants of First Church decided that they needed to help the new people. They want to preach the Gospel to people, but as their pastor says, "We need to earn the right to speak." So they help. They call on people and ask if they can do anything. They are tutoring and helping with educational and food needs. And the joy of serving is changing First Church members. They now see the need for a more solid relationship with God as they face new situations in their outreach to the migrant workers. Church members have had occasional disagreements over all the changes. They are learning to pray more about that and to talk with each other honestly and kindly. It's a steep learning curve, but they're learning!

"You can't give what you don't got—your relationship with God must be hot!"

A Real Life, Non-Vicious Cycle

Do you see how these three sets of relationships work a bit like the Trinity? They are separate, but they are a unity. An individual's relationship with God affects the way s/he works in the church. If many people are praying and becoming more yielded to the Spirit, relationships within the congregation can shift. Then the church feels lighter, more joyful, more real. People want to invite their friends. So friends and new Christians add their own excitement and growth to the mix. Things change again. The changes create a bit of dissonance in the church, so members move into more prayer and work on their relationships. (Chapter 6 deals with some of these issues.)

Growth can start from any one of the three parts of this trinity. A new member with a Pentecostal background can be happy and excited and get some mission projects started. Then people's focus turns outward. They don't obsess over the budget quite as much. Prayer can begin in the session/council/pastor-parish/board/committee meetings, and who knows where Christ can lead from there? The addition of some critical number of new members who are different than the "old" church members usually drives pastors and board members to their knees! Changes are tough. Real church relationships, like a real marriage or a real family, come about through prayer, honesty and attention. Because relationships involve people who are always changing, they *force* you to prayer so you don't smack somebody! As Woody Allen said in *Annie Hall,* "Relationships are like sharks. They have to keep moving, or they die."[4] Growing people are dynamic. Growing churches, comprised of growing people, help transform lives.

DISCUSSION QUESTIONS

1. How is your individual prayer going? Spend the first 10 minutes of your time together sharing the highlights of your prayer time with each other. How have you seen God this week?

2. Does any Bible passage come to mind when you read this chapter? Does one occur to you now? Discuss how it connects with what you have read. (If no passages come to mind, you might want to look at: Mark 12:28–31; Ephesians 4:13–16; Philippians 3:12–16.)

3. How highly does your congregation prioritize a relationship with God?

4. How are relationships in your congregation? With whom in your congregation (besides the pastor) do you talk about what is really going on in your life? How Christlike is the process of decision making in your church? What do you feel best about in the relationships in your church? What could be improved?

5. How strongly do you live out of your faith into your relationships outside church? How many times in the last three months have you had a conversation with an unchurched person about faith?

6. How do these three sets of relationships (with God, within the church, reaching out to others) interact in your church?

At the beginning of each session:

A. Light a candle to remind us of Christ's presence;

B. Repeat aloud, together: **"We agree that we will hold everything shared in this group in complete confidence."**

EXERCISE

It makes a difference if people are actually praying in the church (and *for* the church). Somehow, mysteriously, the church building itself reflects the spiritual health of your congregation. You can help the relationships of the church get healthier with prayer. Start by sitting right where you are in the room you where you meet. First, pray for the whole church. Sit quietly, eyes closed, then imagine your entire church building "shrunk down" to toy sized, and feel it held between your hands. Ask Christ to hold the church, using *your* hands and lap and arms. Ask Christ to send his love through you to heal the church, and all the people in the church, and all the people the church can reach in the next year or two. You may feel dopey doing this. You may feel tingling or heat in your hands. Images or thoughts may pop into your head. Pay attention to what happens. Talk about it with each other.

Next, stand in a big circle around the edge of the room. Close your eyes. Ask Jesus to be in this room, to bless it, to make it a holy place where everyone can grow in faith without distractions. Some of you may feel nudged by the Spirit to move somewhere else in the room. You may want to lay your hand on a chair to bless it, or to make a sign of the cross on the door frame, to stand in a corner and ask God to protect and heal those who enter. If so, do it! Some may feel called to pray that your church's trinity of relationships be healthy and blessed in this room (with God, with each other, with those your church can reach). You may want to pray in silence; you may be moved to speak a few words aloud. Ask the Spirit how you should pray. Then follow the leadings.

Each small group doing this all-congregation study will pray for its own classroom, then for another room or two in your church building. Large groups can split into several "room praying teams!" Don't forget little rooms, bathrooms, storage rooms, the basement, the attic. Pray that every person who enters be there in the Spirit of Christ. Pray that everyone be healed and protected when they enter. (And if you discover a room that looks grubby, organize a little cleaning squad to take care of that in the next week or so!)

Reconvene and talk about what you just did and how it felt. See if the church feels different in the upcoming weeks.

> *Note: Next week's exercise involves homework! Be sure to look ahead tonight while you're together, then do your assignment on page 71 during the week. You'll discuss it when you come back together next week.*

---

[1]My hero, Fred Craddock, New Testament and preaching professor, used the phrase "eating fried preacher for Sunday supper." It was in some sermon one time. There are probably more Craddockisms here. We Disciples pastors compete in sword drills on the Craddock canon. We don't try to plagiarize. It's just that his phrases are integrated into our cells at a submolecular level. Go ahead. Listen to Craddock sermons. Read a collection of his stories. You'll start talking like this, too, and your life will be better. Read *Craddock Stories,* ed. Mike Graves and Richard F. Ward (St. Louis: Chalice Press, 2001).

[2]*Jacobellis v. Ohio,* 878 U.S. 184 (1964).

[3]Please do not hear "unattainable megachurch" when I say "great congregations." Some of these churches have 100 members and are located in tiny towns.

[4]*Annie Hall,* MGM, 1977.

PART TWO

- **PART ONE** focuses on *what is* and on *what can be* for individuals and for churches.

- **PART TWO** helps you see your church more clearly and start to move toward new possibilities.

- **PART THREE** is your 40-day, individual prayer journal. Use it on your own each day. You can discuss it each week when you meet with your study group.

Pray…that God will open to us a door for the word, that we may declare the mystery of Christ, for which I am in prison, so that I may reveal it clearly, as I should. (Col. 4:3–4)

CHAPTER 4

What New Members Want— Transformed Lives

Mel Gibson starred in a movie called *What Women Want*.[1] Gibson was a ladies' man who could suddenly read women's minds. He knew what women, his natural prey, wanted. He knew when to give flowers, when to lean close, when to retreat, ***exactly*** what to say to get the reaction he wanted. He knew what women were thinking! This was going to be ***great!***

The problems started when he learned what women were thinking. He could hear them think about what a jerk he was, about their loneliness. When he actually started listening, he changed. He didn't have to go to crazy extremes like talking about feelings during the Super Bowl, but it got close.

Mel Gibson is to women as churches are to church visitors. Perhaps not consciously, but under the smooth surface, a lot of us secretly look at new members as prey. Think of all the times you've heard, or said, "We need new members with children." "If we had more new members, we could meet this budget." "We have taught Sunday School all these years. It's time for some young women to take their turns." No matter that many of those young women have never been in Sunday School themselves. We need…we need…Ouch. That's new members as prey.

It is so easy to slip into the mind-set of a "church leader." We church leaders carry crucial responsibilities for the institution that is the church. Church financial secretaries and treasurers don't take money or budgets lightly. Nor should they! As council members,

He found the key, the secret combination, the hidden core of the heart of ministry. "***All I had to do was get people whose life Jesus had changed to get up and tell people about it.***" Once we understand that the faith is about transformed lives, once we let the people talk about it in their own words, hearts will be touched and lives will be changed, including ours.

elders, trustees, members of committees, we are called to support the health of our churches. Inevitably, we focus on those jobs.

But our focus can get like a camera that's zoomed in too far. We miss the big picture. We forget that the larger purpose of the church is to take the Gospel out beyond the walls. We begin to see new members as fresh hands, energy and wallets to help keep the church going. We're not mean-spirited. We all do it. We just laser in on an important job and lose sight of that big picture…

Through the Eyes of Two Pastors

We found little difference between the opinions and perceptions of old and of young people who had been raised in the church. The real differences appeared between people who were raised in the church and those who weren't.

Pastor 1: The other day I received a letter from a brilliant young pastor. Jim has just moved from his first call as an associate pastor to his first senior pastor position. He is thrilled. His description was as sweet-spirited as it could be: "I can't believe what it feels like to look into the faces of these children and think that I'll be able to help teach them about Jesus and then baptize them. And the adults are wonderful. They've been so welcoming to Sarah and me. I see these old ones and want to know their stories. I wonder if I will be part of their final transition into a full life with God. The thought of summing up their lives in a funeral sermon overwhelms me. I know I am to be here, and I am so grateful to God for leading us here."

Jim could not have been clearer about his love (Christ's love!) for these people. But do you hear what is missing? Read his letter again. Do you see what is **not** there? *He goes through every age group, but never mentions anyone outside the church.* He shows no consciousness of those beyond the walls. He displays no sense of mission.

Jim is already concentrating on his job, his call, his church. This narrowing of focus is a huge risk for every one of us. This insider-focus is chaplaincy. It is not the vibrant ministry of the Gospel. The danger of that mind-set, sweet-spirited as it may be, is that it focuses on the church as an end in itself. This inward-focused perception leads to thinking of new members as cogs to fill slots, to do jobs. This perception lets us forget that visitors are precious souls who may or may not know God.

Pastor 2: At the beginning of the study, I spoke with a great Methodist pastor who had spent years thinking like Jim. Luke grew up a Methodist boy, became a Methodist college student, a Methodist man, a Methodist pastor. He is brilliant, funny and loving. The churches he served grew rapidly. Parishioners loved him. He was completely charged about ministry. This is the kind of guy we would **all** love to have as our pastor.

Then his bishop asked if Luke would start a new church in a quickly growing suburban area. He said, "Sure, why not?" And he started. Several months into church planting, he looked around and wondered, "Where are all the **Methodists**? All my life there have been Methodists. They're the ones who know what to do and who do all the work. Where **are** they? What am I going to **do**?"

He described the pain of this moment. "I realized that I had unconsciously presumed that there were only two ways to become a Methodist. You either were born one, or you married one."

It took three more months for Luke to figure out what to do. "It's so embarrassing that it took this long, but I spent three months drifting, trying harder. Then it all fell into place. It's completely simple. All I had to do was get someone whose life Jesus had changed to get up and tell people about it. Then I just sat back and clipped coupons. I supported them when they got great ideas."

Over 800 people were worshiping in that new church eight or nine years later, when the bishop asked him to do something else. His associate minister and many church members told stories that suggest he was doing a lot more than clipping coupons and eating bonbons on the divan. This guy worked hard. He preached great sermons, trained teams, encouraged and supported people who felt prompted by the Spirit to start ministries. Several high school kids got this computer/Internet idea. He encouraged them to develop their idea to huge results.

However, Luke was right. He found the key, the secret combination, the hidden core of the heart of ministry. *"All I had to do was get people whose life Jesus had changed to get up and tell people about it."* Once we understand that the faith is about transformed lives, and let the people talk about it in their own words, hearts will be touched, lives will be changed, including ours. Then ministry doesn't feel like pushing rocks up hill. It's standing on the top and letting the rocks roll down. When we finally see that the faith is about our lives being changed by Jesus, we no longer think of new members as prey. We think of their stories.

> Generally, the newer the Christian, the more important the relationships with people as they discover it's God they're looking for. Whether children or adults, most of us first learn about God's love through other people.

Through the Eyes of the Unchurched

This chapter is about those stories. Let's hear from the people whose lives Jesus has changed. What do they think? What do they want? What do they see? What needs do they have? Let's not try to anticipate. Let's listen!

Have you ever talked with people who joined their church recently, or who have just become a Christian? We discovered that when new members, particularly new Christians, talk about their new churches, their answers cluster into two areas:

1. they feel loved, accepted and comfortable in the church, and
2. they are learning about God (Jesus, Spirit) and growing spiritually.

Same "Trinity of Relationships," from a Different Perspective

Do those new members' answers sound familiar? They should. Remember the three main characteristics of health we found in churches that are doing the best jobs of evangelism? These churches have a healthy "trinity of relationships" (individual relationships with God, healthy relationships between church members and a love for people outside the church, see chapter 5). The church members understand what it's like for God to transform their lives. They tell people outside the church walls. New members in these churches understand two things best: that God loves them and the church loves them. That's effective evangelism! Understand the Gospel, live it out, convey it accurately to new people. The new people understand it. That's as good as it gets!

The important thing to remember for us as insiders is that we see these three aspects of a healthy church from a "churched" perspective. New members see a loving church and learn about God through a different lens. The newer the Christian, the more differently they talk about church than do long-time members.

A big surprise came out of the statistical part of the Mainline Evangelism Project. We found little difference between the opinions and perceptions of old and of young people who had been raised in the church. The real differences appeared between people who were raised in the church and those who weren't.

If you grew up in the church, no matter how cool and young you are, don't assume you know what people outside the church are thinking or what they want! Early in your life, you absorbed Christian theology, behaviors, values, and understandings. These unconscious influences shape the way you think about life and what's real. If you want to know what nonchurch people think or what they expect, you have to ask them. Don't presume that you know.

"I was living a sinful, no meaning life with no real direction. I had just ended a ten-year relationship that I was trying to get over. As I struggled through depression, anxiety, and bad thoughts, God kept calling out to me. I would often have religious thoughts even though I did not understand what true religion was. I knew my life was a mess and I was ready or in the process of giving up. My friend who cuts my hair knew of my unhappiness but not the details. She invited me to [the UCC church I joined], and from that moment I knew I had been given a second chance with my life. I now live a simple, wholesome life and love every minute of it."

Think of it this way: Church is like comfort food. What's comfort food for you? Is it the tuna noodle casserole with peas in it and potato chips on top? Burritos? Could it be that green bean casserole with cream of mushroom soup and Durkee's™ onion rings? French's™ yellow mustard on that hotdog or Dijon?™ Do you want Miracle Whip™ or Hellman's™ mayonnaise on your Thanksgiving Friday turkey sandwich? Hershey's,™ M&M's™ or Godiva?™ The one thing we all know is that you don't mess with comfort food! You don't substitute or it's Wrong. We formed our rigid opinions about comfort food in childhood, at the same time our Christian ideas solidified.

Like it or not, the survey found that the opinions of 40-year-olds raised in the church are a lot more like the preferences of 80-year-olds raised in church than they are like 40-year-olds who were **not** raised in the church. If you grew up with liturgy and hymns, you probably feel comfortable with them. You experienced God early in connection with the smells of Easter lilies and the colors of Christmas pageants, with the doxology, hanging banners and the songs you loved from camp.

I don't feel as comfortable in a contemporary worship setting as I do with liturgy. Because of my upbringing and education I'm wired for liturgy. I love Hellman's,™ and I think Miracle Whip™ tastes nasty. A switch from Hellman's™ *worship* to either Miracle Whip™ worship *or* gourmet French mayonnaise worship is a bad thing for me on a grumpy day! I can feel put out by **any** kind of worship that doesn't feel like Hellman's.™ Then I remember: "Oh, phooey. It doesn't always have to be about me! It matters that I'm comfortable, but my comfort isn't as important as that 23-year-old over there whom the kids have been inviting to worship for three months. Pretty amazing he's here."

So, let's try to listen to what some new members of churches are saying. Don't change a thing you're doing. Your worship, your classes may be exactly right for the people God is calling you to reach. For now, let's simply try to *hear* what a few new members are saying.

What Do New Members Say about Churches and Faith?

Here are areas we investigated in our study. You can find more detail on the study at www.GraceNet.info. During the Mainline Evangelism Project, we asked all sorts of new members these questions. Their answers may help you understand how unchurched or non-Christian people think. We asked:

1. Why do people first visit the church they join?

"I grew up never attending church or knowing Jesus. My family started attending after my husband lost his job and we felt something missing in our lives. We wanted our children to be exposed to Sunday School lessons. After attending over a year, I believed that if I just asked God to forgive my sins, I would meet my Savior in heaven."

2. What gets visitors back for a second visit?

3. Why do new members join?

4. At what points in their lives are people most open to becoming involved or re-involved in church?

5. What does conversion/recommitment look like?

6. What aspects of being a Christian are most important to you?

New members' answers to these questions mesh with the "real relationships" discussion in chapter 5. People who join churches want a real relationship with God. They want a real relationship with loving people. Many new Christians discover that they wanted a relationship with God and loving people even before they knew they wanted it. One new Christian told me, "The church helped me see that I was built for God. I didn't know that, because I didn't know much about God and I was so busy being so busy. But [my friends in the church] helped me see what I'd been looking for off and on since I was a kid. Now that I've turned my life over to Christ, I feel like my life makes sense for the first time in 20 years." Generally, the newer the Christian, the more important the relationships with people as they discover it's God they're looking for. Whether children or adults, most of us first learn about God's love through other people.

1. Why Do People First Visit the Church They Join?

Almost 60% of new members of evangelistic churches get there first because a person invited them, or because they know someone in the church. This was one of the clearest findings of our study. Percentages are identical for both new Christians and Christians with a church background. The second place reasons for attending reflect a difference between new Christians and new members who have a church background. New Christians point to an event—a wedding or a funeral. Members with a church background place denominational affiliation in second place. But this second reason weighed in at only 9% in each case.

Both new Christians and new members with a church background said that the biggest barrier to attending the church was not knowing anyone.

Put these two findings together and you will see that the one most effective thing you can do to get evangelism going in your church is to invite people to church!

One woman told us about a tough transition time in her life. She talked with six friends about what was going on in her life. One

"Both my wife and myself must have felt the Spirit at the same time. When my sister-in-law invited us to an Easter Service, we both had a feeling it was something we wanted to try. I think David's greeting and words touched something in us. We felt compelled to come back. Each service left us feeling better and opened a new door for me. I think it was the first time I ever felt the Lord's presence."

Saturday night she decided to try a church. On Sunday morning, she walked into a congregation close to her house. She was shocked to find five of the six people she'd talked to sitting in the sanctuary! Not one of them had suggested that church might help. She had no idea that any of them were even members of a church. She didn't know they were Christians.

2. What Gets Visitors Back?

What gets visitors back for second, third, fourth visits to a church? The people are the factor cited by 38% of new Christians and 30% of new members with a church background who say they return repeatedly because of the warmth, the love, the "realness" of the church members. *The pastor* is the second most frequently mentioned reason for returning to the church after initial visits (28% for new Christians, 23% for people with a church background). Also, 14% of new members say they returned because of worship.

Doctrine, theology and denominational affiliation matter to only 5% of the people with a church background and were not mentioned at all by the new Christians. It is interesting to note a seeming paradox. While 60% of new members say they visited the first time because of an invitation or because of knowing someone in the church, knowing someone in the church is only mentioned by 4% of new members as the reason for coming *back* to the church.

So, an invitation seems to get these visitors there in the first place, but the welcome, warmth and authenticity of people; the personality, teaching and preaching of the pastor and worship bring visitors *back* to experience church life again.

"God is so great. There is so much to learn and receive from him. The church is a very important part in growing your faith with God. My church is full of loving and caring people. I feel welcome every time I walk through the door by the smiles and the beautiful cross in the front of the sanctuary."

3. Why Do New Members Join a Church?

By the time people get to a point of making a firm commitment to Christ and the church, they have moved more deeply into faith issues. The following are the top reasons mentioned (in percentages of total responses) by new members of the highly evangelistic churches. We asked them to fill in the blank for the question, "What made you ready to join *this* church?"[2]

At the point of joining a new church, the reasons are much more about what's going on in lives, and less about the first issues of being comfortable and feeling welcomed. First-time visitors need an invitation to get in the door. Visitors come back because of the warmth of members, the pastor and what they are learning.

MOTIVATION	New Christians	Church Background
Something was missing in my life	36%	27%
I'd been thinking religious things for a long time	16%	12%
Family/children motivations	17%	19%
Growth of relationship with God or Jesus	10%	18%
A birth or death	15%	2%
Want to be part of church (includes be part of church family, to serve, need to belong, support)	6%	14%

"It's been a long and arduous journey so far. I would say it started with the death of my brother when I was 15. That left me in a deep void and started my search for the unanswered questions and feelings I had."

At the point of joining, however, look how even the human relationships drop to the bottom of the list. New members are particularly thinking about questions about the meaning of their lives, like "What is missing in my life?" In the written comments, new Christians usually point to missing a relationship with God, but also describe some aspects of a maturing faith. New members with church backgrounds usually don't say that something was missing from their lives. That is not surprising. They already have some sort of faith life. The established Christians point instead to growth of their relationship with God or Jesus.

4. When Are People Most Open to Start Coming to Church?

The typical story from new Christians and from new members who have not been involved in church for a while starts with a transition. ***People are most open to becoming involved with Christ and a church during seasons of change in their lives.*** It can be good change (marriage, birth of a child, a physical move) or a painful change (illness, death of someone dear, divorce, loss of a job), but disruption in our lives seems to be a natural point at which people are open to a life change.

A church treasurer, a normal, quiet CPA named Brian, told me, "It's hard for me to be outgoing or really friendly like some people, so what I do is to pray that God will show me people to pray for who might be open to Christ now. When I ask, God brings people to my mind, or into my life, whose kids left for college a couple months before. Sometimes it's someone who just retired, or a lady whose husband just died, or someone who lost his job. When their names come into my mind, I call them for lunch or golf and then I ask them if they want to come to church. I don't talk about a lot of stuff, but I invite them."

I asked Brian what has happened with the people he has invited to church. He said, "Well, a lot of them have come to church, and a large percentage of them have joined. I really never have been able to tell them about the Lord or lead them to Christ or through the steps of salvation or all that, I just tell them church means a lot to me and helps me. I guess my job's just the praying and the inviting."

5. What Are the Most Important Parts of Being a Christian?

We asked new members of the high baptism churches, "Which of the following aspects of being a Christian are most significant in your own life?" New Christians and new members with church backgrounds gave almost identical answers when we asked them to identify the most important aspects of being a Christian:

A. "My sins are forgiven."

B. "It gives meaning and purpose to my life."

C. "It gives me a relationship with God/Jesus."

D. "I have eternal life."[3]

The least significant answer out of 11 possibilities for both groups was, "It saves me from Hell."

New faith or renewed faith is personal. It's deep. These new church members pointed out the four deepest elements of faith from a list of 11 options. These four aspects of faith the new members chose are some of the most profound issues of existence with which the faith has grappled over the ages. Faith is affecting the depths of these new members' lives.

Occasionally you hear Christians say that the churches that are doing evangelism are "shallow" or "selling out the Gospel" or "catering to what people want, not what they need." Our study showed something very different. We saw that the people who are pouring themselves into evangelism are thinking deeply about the heart of the faith and doing everything they can to convey those realities to people who do not know God.

New Christians usually don't sound like theology professors. But we have seen many new Christians gravitating to deep faith realities—love for God and yieldedness to God. Interviews and surveys reveal that the new members are learning to talk about their faith clearly, biblically, theologically. They are feeling their faith and are living it.

"My becoming a Christian was more of a journey than an event. I prayed for and received guidance and strength along the way. This journey has continued to my current church and my continued development as a Christian who spreads the word."

Eternal life with God matters to new Christians. Hell isn't mentioned, but the thought of Hell motivates many Christians who share their faith. Twelve hundred interviews, congregational visits and the written surveys point to the same thing. Effective evangelistic people and churches have deep faith and comfort in their understanding of eternal life with God. They do not stress Hell in preaching or teaching, but many of them have a classical biblical understanding of Hell and therefore are motivated by it.

New Christians usually come to churches as theological clean slates. Our culture does a great job of conveying vivid images of Hell on Earth, but Americans may be shakier on the eternal kind! I suspect that most unchurched Americans don't think much about Hell. Once exposed to Christian preaching, teaching and biblical understandings, new Christians can learn about Hell and think more about eternity. But scaring people about Hell is not helpful for most Americans. Ruined lives, uncertainty, exhaustion, addictions, a treadmill existence or concern for their children seem to be more important entry points for the Gospel today.

> Most unchurched Americans don't think much about Hell. Ruined lives, uncertainty, exhaustion, addictions, a treadmill existence or concern for their children seem to be more important entry points for the Gospel today.

6. What Does Conversion/Recommitment Look Like?

We will have more to say about this (see "Bandwidths of Evangelism" in chapter 5). Here is the highlight: people who were not raised in the church are different. They may not know the story of baby Jesus in the manger. Words like *grace, redemption, original sin*—or the books of the Bible—may be completely unknown. Unchurched Baby Boomers may think that *Amazing Grace* is a Judy Collins song and that Cat Stevens wrote *Morning Has Broken*. I have heard three different people say that they only know one hymn, "that one about dew on roses and walking in the garden with Jesus. They sang it at my grandmother's funeral."

The great news about this is that the mysterious words of faith have not been worn slick by use. Reading the Bible is like reading Shakespeare for the first time, "Whoa! Is *that* where this comes from?" The hard news for us is that we can't communicate well through the theological words or concepts that we've worked so hard to learn and now take for granted! We need to know how to talk about Jesus from our own lives, out of our real feelings of faith and doubt, and in real-life words.

What do conversions look like? It's hard for most church people to imagine. It's not about church, it's about Jesus. It's about one human being, at a crucial point in his or her life, learning about God being love and about Jesus being God. Then s/he decides to live life with

God leading. Some people come to Christ through their feelings—in response to a change, a crisis, a loss, a new joy like the birth of a baby. Others have important or complex intellectual questions answered.

One man with a church background transferred membership. Two years later, he responded to the question, "Why did you join *this* church?" this way:

> It is an outward-looking church. It is very involved in the community. It is not moralistic or legalistic but rather invites me to a personal struggle towards God and Jesus while supporting me in the midst of a community of believers. It's not a homogenous church in terms of belief, but the disagreements I've seen or heard of seemed to serve to enrich the faith of all rather than demoralize them. My faith is sustained and defined by social justice in the name of Christ and this church is actively engaged in the same struggle.

Do you hear his appreciation of the church? He is growing spiritually. The fit between his well-formed faith and the church is clear. You probably know people who have joined your church who sound like this. They have chosen your church. They probably bring fresh life to the congregation. And they are happy to continue their Christian growth there.

Now, listen to new Christians talk about becoming Christians and joining their churches. Hear the freshness in their tones of voice. Sometimes they sound theologically naive. Sometimes they show tremendous sophistication. They almost always sound grateful, in love with Christ and their church. I am usually awed by the power of new Christians' grasp of the supernatural and of the center of the faith—their love of God. How do you respond to these statements from new Christians?

- "I am too new to active Christianity to be able to add meaningful comment. However, for me, I believe that the only way to God is through my Lord Jesus Christ. In believing in the Christ as my Lord, it becomes important to me to try to change my life to become more like Him."
- "I became involved in church again for the first time since childhood. My life was so fun and so full. I was taking care of the twins, running them around to their activities, doing my job, keeping house. I went along like that for years. Then Ed had this affair that broke my heart. No, not just my heart. It broke my life. And my neighbor Sandy was incredible. She listened and listened. She helped me pay bills and cook when I couldn't

> "I was an alcoholic and drug addict. I went to order a pizza one night and misdialed the number. The person at the other end of the phone was a pastor from [the church I ended up joining]. I received Christ the next day. Since then I have known the joy and love of Christ. Later, I went on a short missionary trip to Cuba that made me realize how much God wants us to share his message."

even function. She prayed for me. I'd prayed before, but this was different. I felt as if there really was a Jesus and he was standing right there with his arm around my shoulders. I mean it was really Sandy's arm, but it felt like Jesus'. That was the start."

■ "I never knew intellectual Christians. Actually, in the last two years since I began attending [my church], I realize I probably *have* known intelligent, liberal Christians, but I didn't know they *were* Christians. This congregation is amazing. The people are thoughtful. They have a variety of ways set up to serve people in our city. We have a reading program and a food bank. A group of us monitor legislation during the state legislative session. Different beliefs are represented in this church, but they have ability to discuss issues openly. I find no dogmatic, simplistic, theological strictures. I am beginning to develop an interest in the spiritual disciplines, which is completely new for me."

■ "I grew up in Indiana. After marriage I went to Iran. I was in an abusive marriage, and my husband would not allow me to see my children for two years. That is legal in Iran, and the courts would not allow me to see them. My husband accused me of crimes for which I was scared I might be stoned to death. I fled the country. After coming here, I felt drawn to Christ from my childhood Catholic schools in Indiana. I tried many churches here and ended up at First Christian. Here the Bible study taught me about God and the church helped me get political asylum." (Her children, ages 8 and 12 as I write this, are still in Iran.)

■ "Being frustrated by the other churches I tried, I thought about Mr. Rogers and the qualities he stood for. I found them here."[4]

New Christians have fresh faith. They appreciate their new church homes as much as new members with a church background. But these new Christians help us see a fresh faith, a new faith. Did you ever have a time in your life of first love for Christ? How did you feel about your first church? How do those early feelings compare to your faith today? Have you grown in love and in understanding?

DISCUSSION QUESTIONS _____

1. How is your individual prayer going? Spend the first 10 minutes of your time together sharing the highlights of your prayer time with each other. How have you seen God this week?

2. Did any Bible passage come to mind as you read this chapter? Does one occur to you now? Discuss how it connects with what

---

The one most effective thing you can do to get evangelism going in your church is to invite people to church!

At the beginning of each session:

A. Light a candle to remind us of Christ's presence;

B. Repeat aloud, together: **"We agree that we will hold everything shared in this group in complete confidence."**

you have read. (If no passages come to mind, you might want to look at: Luke 15; Acts 10:9–16; Ephesians 2:11–22; Philippians 2:3–4.)

3. Did you ever have a time of first being in love with God? How does that time compare with your feelings and understandings today? Have you lost anything? What have you gained in your faith?

4. Have you participated in helping Christ transform someone else's life? Who have you invited to church? When was the last time you welcomed a visitor? Helped organize a dinner for visitors? Talked with someone about your relationship with God or about asking God to lead your life? Prayed for someone to come to know Jesus? What happened?

5. What are your church's stories about people whose lives God has transformed as a result of your church's ministry, or because of the actions of Christians in your church?

> We need to know how to talk about Jesus from our own lives, out of our real feelings of faith and doubt—in real life words.

EXERCISE _____

During this week, will you each interview *either* a person who used to go to church but doesn't attend now, *OR* someone with no church background at all? You may have to hunt for these people, but look among coworkers, neighbors, your grandchildren's high-school friends, a nurse friend, the clerk at the hardware store. Keep in mind that you're doing an interview to find out their opinions, so they'll probably be flattered to be asked and listened to, not threatened!

Explain that you and some of your friends in your church are trying to figure out ways to help your church be even more open to new people. Tell them that you have been a Christian for so long and love your church so much, you don't have a good perspective on it anymore. Let them know that you have decided to do interviews with people who aren't in the middle of things at church so that you can get a better perspective.

Over lunch or coffee, ask the following questions. LISTEN until they stop talking! Take notes. Ask follow-up questions if it seems appropriate. Don't give advice or give answers. Just get their opinions. Try to hear not only what they say, but how they say it. Listen for what they *don't* say.

1. What pops into your mind when you hear the word *church*?

2. Has anyone ever invited you to their church? What did you think when they asked you? Did you go? How did it feel? If you didn't go, why not?

3. Have you ever had a sense of God or Jesus communicating with you? What was it like?

4. If you had one question you could ask God and knew you'd get an answer, what would it be?

5. Would you like prayer for anything? (You may pray there, if it's private and they're comfortable with that, or tell them you'll be praying for them during your prayer times. If they have asked for prayer, call them back in a week or so. Ask how the situation's going and if there's any different way you could focus your prayer for them. You may be the only person praying for them.)

What do conversions look like? It's hard for most church people to imagine. It's not about church, it's about Jesus.

Come back and share what you discovered with the people in your group. Were there similarities? Did the age or experience of the people interviewed make a difference? Did anyone in your group interview anyone with a tattoo? Someone with a different racial, economic or educational background than the majority of your church members? Did you end up inviting them to your church? If not, why not? While you are together, pray for each of these people you interviewed.

If You Want to Go Further

Many books are available to help you think further about helping Christ transform people's lives by becoming Christian or becoming active in a great church. Some of the best are George Hunter's *Church for the Unchurched* and *The Celtic Way of Evangelism* (both from Abingdon Press) and Brian McLaren's *A New Kind of Christian* (Jossey-Bass).

---

[1] *What Women Want,* Paramount, 2000.

[2] These percentages do not add up to 100% because many people gave more than one reason for joining when they wrote why they joined the church. These are the percentages of the total number of times people described something that fit in these top categories.

[3] Reasons C and D are in different order for new and "established" Christians. New Christians list eternal life as the third reason and empowerment by the Holy Spirit and connection with the Divine as almost equal in fourth place. For details, see full report at www.GraceNet.info.

[4] Fred Rogers, a quiet, cardigan-wearing Presbyterian minister, was the central figure of PBS's longest-running show, *Mister Rogers' Neighborhood.* Generations of children, from the mid-1960s through today, loved our gentle, kindly neighbor.

CHAPTER 5

How's Your Church Doing?

Bandwidths, Barriers and Bridges

Four years of talking with over 1200 people about evangelism brought several surprises. One of the biggest is the amount of guilt people feel about not doing much evangelism. The worst problem with guilt is that it can shut down clear thinking. It can also stop action. Most congregations ARE doing at least some evangelism, in many cases, good evangelism! So let's focus on what we are doing, then open up more bridges to the unchurched.

This chapter focuses on three things:

1. *"Bandwidths of Evangelism"*—nine different kinds of people to reach

2. *"Barriers to Evangelism"*—things that block us from sharing the Gospel

3. *"Bridges into Your Church"*—passageways to build for new members

Bandwidths of Evangelism

Remember your fourth-grade science teacher explaining how radios are tuned? Radio stations broadcast on different frequencies, different "bandwidths" of the airwaves. Let's think about evangelism as one big broadcasting of the Great Commission. Remember Jesus' final meeting with the disciples just before he ascended into heaven? Matthew's gospel reports Jesus' last words to the disciples:

Many Christians feel guilty about not doing much evangelism. The worst problem with guilt is that it can shut down clear thinking. It can also stop action.

Now the eleven disciples went to Galilee, to the mountain to which Jesus had directed them. When they saw him, they worshiped him; but some doubted. And Jesus came and said to them, "All authority in heaven and on earth has been given to me. Go therefore and make disciples of all nations, baptizing them in the name of the Father and of the Son and of the Holy Spirit, and teaching them to obey everything that I have commanded you. And remember, I am with you always, to the end of the age. (Mt. 28:16–20)

All nations! All authority! Everything I have commanded you! To the end of the Age! *That's* daunting. This is part of the problem. We see the big picture, get scared, and the guilt takes control. We decide if we're not converting Africa single-handedly that we're not doing evangelism. (Actually, Africa is sending us missionaries now, and thank God for it!) We feel guilt and we forget to invite our next-door neighbor to church on Sunday. Surely we can find some middle ground in between those two extremes.

For this book, let's agree on the vital importance of our connections with the entire world. Let's agree to go on mission trips in the U.S. and abroad and send money to missions in other countries. But for the purposes of this chapter, we will think of evangelism in terms of the people on your doorsteps with whom you and your congregation can share your excitement about your faith. The purpose of rethinking evangelism isn't to water down some definition. It's to help us be sensitive to opportunities that surround us.

You probably don't think of working with some of these people as evangelism. For this "bandwidths of evangelism" idea, ask two questions:

1. Are we helping this person move into relationship with God?
2. Are we helping this person move into Christian community?

If the answer to either question is yes, we are going to call it evangelism, the sharing of the Gospel. Here are some bandwidths on which your church may already be broadcasting its message of the love of God:

Bandwidth 101.1–Children and Youth of the Congregation. Who is closest to you, to your church, who doesn't fully know God through Christ? The children of your congregation. Think of every Sunday School class, every youth group meeting as a way to help our children know Jesus and learn the power of being part of the church. When they get old enough to make decisions for their own

---

Is It Evangelism?

1. Are we helping this person move into relationship with God?
2. Are we helping this person move into Christian community?

If the answer to either question is yes, we are going to call it evangelism, the sharing of the Gospel.

lives, they will be able to make choices, knowing the options. Most of the people who join churches as adults were raised in the church. Working with our own children is evangelism.

Bandwidth 101.2–Children and Youth's Friends. Our children have friends at school and in their neighborhoods. Inviting them and helping them get to church activities is evangelism. Many current church members and pastors did not grow up in the church with their families. A grandparent, a family friend, a neighbor, a godparent, a Sunday School teacher brought them to church.

Bandwidth 101.3–People Attached to Your Church Who

Bandwidths of Evangelism

101.1
our children

101.2
our children's friends

101.3
attenders, not committed

101.4
transfers, similar theology

101.5
transfers, different theology

101.6
far from church, drifted

101.7
far from church, hurt

101.8
not Christian, similar

101.9
not Christian, different

Never Joined. Look closely at your congregation. You will discover people who attend church (steady visitors, relatives of a committed member, people with mental or physical disabilities) but who have never joined it or never offered their lives to Christ. Some of them have been connected with the congregation and served in various capacities for decades! When invited to be baptized or to join the church, they are often grateful and enthusiastic. Making a decision to be baptized or join a congregation can provide a life-changing boost in spiritual growth and involvement in the church. It's also life-giving for the person who extends the invitation!

Bandwidth 101.4–Committed Christians from Similar Church Backgrounds. Devoted Christians move to your town from other cities. They tend to start visiting neighborhood churches in their denomination, but denominational loyalty is not as strong a force as it once was (chapter 4). The younger they are, the more Christians are willing to move to a church of similar theology and cultural feel. New transfer members point to something that "felt right" about the new church they ended up joining. They are often drawn to what they loved most about their old church: commitment to Habitat and outreach, strong Bible teaching, a social justice focus, a specific type of worship, or speaking in tongues. These are some of the easiest people to help move into your church's life. They show up and if it feels like a good fit to them, if you're friendly and structured to assimilate new members easily, they join!

Bandwidth 101.5–Committed Christians from <u>Different</u> Church Backgrounds. Bandwidth 101.5 evangelism involves bigger jumps than the church changes in Bandwidth 101.4. These people must make a theological, and usually a denominational, shift. Do you know UCC members who have moved from a congregation with progressive theology to a Nazarene church? Has a family from a noninstrumental Church of Christ church joined your liberal Lutheran congregation? These are cases of Bandwidth 101.5 evangelism. This bandwidth more often contains a conversion element because the theological underlayment of the two churches is different.

Bandwidth 101.6–People Raised in the Church Who Drifted Away. We all know people who have church backgrounds, believe in God, but who are not committed to a congregation. No big rupture happened. They just drifted away. Often these disassociations from church happened during a time of change: going to college, a move, a job change, a divorce or other crisis, the children moving out and leaving the nest empty. Bandwidth 101.6 people may feel urges to visit a church again during life changes, when a friend talks about loving his church, or if they are invited to a church event. These people's biggest resistance to the idea of church is inertia.

Bandwidth 101.7–People Raised in the Church Who Were Hurt. Think of all the people you know who have had a bad experience with a church or a disillusionment in their faith. The list of types of people the church has wounded is impressive:

    a. ex-church leaders burned out by congregational conflict

    b. adults who were sexually molested by a church leader as a child

    c. women who experienced fundamentalist theology as oppressive

    d. people who lived through a traumatic death or tragedy that triggered a faith crisis (Frequently phrased as, "If God could let something like this happen, I don't want to have anything to ***do*** with God!")

    e. people who felt "shunned" by churches that judged them

    f. let's admit it—some people were so bored by church that they gave up on it!

Many mainline congregations excel at working with people who have been hurt. Be aware that it is generally best to try only once

---

For this chapter, think of evangelism in terms of the people on your doorsteps with whom you and your congregation can share your excitement about your faith. The purpose of rethinking evangelism isn't to water down some definition. It's to help us be sensitive to opportunities that surround us.

to reincorporate former members of your *own* church who were wounded. If they are not ready to return, it is likely God can reach them best through another congregation.

Bandwidth 101.8–Unchurched People <u>Like</u> Current Church Members. A growing number of people have had little or no exposure to Christianity or to churches. They were not raised in the church. They have not been baptized. They are not Christians. They may actually **think** of themselves as Christians, because they live in America and think of all Americans as Christians, so long as they aren't Jewish or Muslim. Millions of people are like this. They may have TV or movie images of Christianity. They may have hostility against the church or vague "pro-faith" feelings even though they know little about it. They are like the members of your congregation in terms of jobs, schooling and ethnicity. Most mainline churches are doing very little to reach these people.

Do you see that most churches are doing some kind of evangelism, some type of sharing of the Good News?

Bandwidth 101.9–Unchurched People <u>Different</u> from Current Church Members. Everything said about the last bandwidth (101.8) applies to this last group of people, but they are different than most of your congregation's members. Imagine a church of primarily upper-middle-class African-Americans evangelizing recent Chinese immigrants who have moved into the neighborhood. Envision a predominantly blue-collar Caucasian congregation working with Hispanic attorneys and professors. This is bandwidth 101.9 evangelism.

Review these bandwidths of evangelism. Do you suspect intuitively that they get more difficult as they progress from 101.1 to 101.9? Does your instinct tell you that it would probably be harder to evangelize a man angry at his old church than to help a happy 10-year-old in your Sunday School class grow in her faith? If so, your intuitions are right on target! In one way, the radio dial drawing at the beginning of this section is misleading. A more accurate way of picturing the bandwidths of evangelism is to stack them on top of each other in a pyramid. This "evangelism pyramid" gives us a better way to see the relative size and difficulty of the bandwidths:

As the pyramid gets skinnier nearer the top, helping the people connect with a church or become Christian gets harder and harder. In addition, the numbers of people added to the church in each of these ways also gets smaller as the pyramid gets up to its point.[1]

Your Church and the Evangelism Bandwidths

All right, how can you think about your congregation's evangelism using the bandwidth pyramid? Start at the bottom of that pyramid

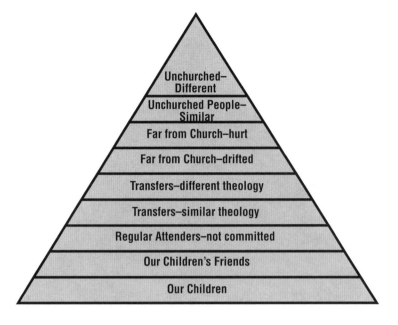

Sometimes these evangelistic movements start with a great idea and careful planning. Sometimes events or relationships percolate and evangelism begins to happen spontaneously. Prayerful people see God's hand in it and figure out next steps to keep participating in what God has started.

and see how many of these kinds of evangelism you're doing, or are on the verge of doing. Why think you have to leap to the top of the pyramid to be doing any evangelism? You don't start playing the violin by launching into the Tchaikovsky concerto. You begin with *Twinkle, Twinkle, Little Star*. Little League kids learn to pitch the ball, to catch the ball, to hit the ball. We start where we are, then add a new challenge.

Do you see that most churches are doing **some** kind of evangelism, **some** type of sharing of the Good News? Do you really believe that God is crazy about us and wants a relationship with us? Almost any congregation is working with its own children—to teach them to love Jesus, who loves them! Almost all of our congregations are doing something to help their children know that the church loves them and to help their children and youth enter into a relationship with Christ that will last forever. That's the start. Where do you go from there? Take two steps:

1. Do what you're doing well a little better

2. Pray to see one new area of evangelism the Spirit would like you to try next

Look at the bandwidths in the pyramid. A logical starting place to focus the congregation's energies may leap out at you. Do the children in your youth group go to the middle school next door to the church? You may be ready for Bandwidth 101.2. Do you have adults with gifts and a call to work with a tutoring program for children? Old basketball players? Ballroom dancing maniacs? A nursing home nearby? Quilters? Ties to the business community?

Think about:

- deep needs of people in your neighborhood
- logical opportunities to meet new people
- the gifts and passions of people in your congregations

If you think about these three: needs, opportunities and gifts, you may find yourself zeroing in on a bandwidth that's logical and feels right.

A Mennonite congregation began teaching Hispanic migrant workers and new Hispanic residents to read. These quiet, intellectual Mennonites found themselves telling their new neighbors stories about Jesus loving them. Many of the tutoring students have been baptized and joined the church. A Disciples of Christ congregation in Oklahoma started a ministry to mentally handicapped people because a brother and sister from a residential home in the neighborhood showed up at church one day. They were baptized and joined the church. They brought their friends. They invited their social workers. A second service started. An ex-prisoner ministry began.

Sometimes these evangelistic movements start with a great idea and careful planning. Sometimes events or relationships percolate and evangelism begins to happen spontaneously. Prayerful people see God's hand in it and figure out next steps to keep participating in what God has started. The pastor of the Oklahoma Disciples church later shook her head, grinned and described the beginnings of the new ministry: "I try to be an organized person. I wish telling all this sounded better! There was something about trying to follow what the Spirit was doing that always felt as if we didn't quite have a plan and I was just punting." In California, pastors say following the Spirit feels like surfing—you catch the next wave God's bringing along. It takes a Sooner to express the follow-the-Spirit feel for many of the rest of us. We who don't live on a coast feel like we're punting!

Another congregation was full of golfers—imagine! They decided to invite unchurched friends to play golf. Conversations began. So did conversions to Christianity.

What is your ministry setting? Who are your church members? What are their interests and gifts? What is already happening with outreach in your church? Pray. Ask God to give you ideas. Discuss them. Keep praying. When it's time, do something. Just keep God in the loop!

Where to start? Think:

1. needs of neighbors
2. opportunities to meet them
3. your gifts and passions

Barriers to Evangelism, Bridges into the Church

Can you see the Lincoln Memorial in your mind's eye? Can you picture that long, shallow flight of steps in front? The building is wide, beautiful and inviting. Picnickers sit on the steps, laughing together or thinking as they gaze into the reflecting pool. You look at that building, glimpse the statue of Lincoln from afar and want to glide toward him.

Now envision a medieval castle. See high walls rising out of that smelly moat. Look up at the crenelations (the bumps on top). Archers shoot arrows or pour hot oil on intruders from between them. The drawbridge is up. The huge wooden door, studded with metal spikes, is closed.

Some of us, as individuals, are as warm, open and welcoming as the Lincoln Memorial. Others of us are like a medieval fortress, bristling with defenses. The same goes for our churches. Some welcome and assimilate new members easily, joyously. Others are draped with barbed wire.

There *is* great news: God is in the business of healing us and our churches, Christ will stand at our elbow and point out our entrenched positions, our towering battlements and those legions of yeomen who are always re-tipping arrows and heating oil. The Spirit can lead us to drain moats, open drawbridges, and build wheelchair-accessible bridges!

We slam the door shut on the Gospel, but Christ opens windows in individual lives and in churches. A pastor named Sally said that she was overwhelmed one morning by St. Paul's explanation of a passage of Isaiah. Paul wrote to the Christians in Rome, "Thus I make it my ambition to proclaim the good news, not where Christ has already been named, so that I do not build on someone else's foundation, but as it is written, 'Those who have never been told of him shall see, / and those who have never heard of him shall understand'" (Rom. 15:20–21).

Sally lived with Paul's words for weeks. She said the Spirit started showing her tiny ways she blocked God from helping her reach out to people who were not yet Christians. "I kept having to ask God's forgiveness every time He showed me another little habit of never thinking to share my faith, or of deflecting faith discussions when I was away from church people. I was mortified. I wasn't talking about Christ unless I was being paid to do it! Finally I went to our elders and told them about it. We prayed together and they had the same sense of conviction I had. We realized we never talked about our

Two types of barriers prevent us from doing effective evangelism: barriers inside our heads, and barriers in the church. Both can block people out.

faith except to each other, in church. It started us on a long journey. We had to rethink almost everything we were doing. We weren't talking about our faith. We realized we were discouraging visitors who hadn't been raised Lutheran. We had never thought of all the little ways our worship and our educational classes made unchurched people feel awkward or ignorant. Why had we assumed that being nice was enough?

"The evangelism minister on our bishop's staff helped us take a fresh look at our hospitality, our worship and our ways of discipling new members. He was great. He kept telling us to *try* things, to experiment. He said loads of our ideas wouldn't work, but just to try a whole lot of different things. We did. Some things flopped. The two big changes we've kept are the contemporary worship service and a coffee shop ministry for teens we're doing with two other churches."

Several years after the Spirit prompted Sally with Romans 15, she said, "The new members have helped, the new Christians especially. We can ask them to help us see how we can be more sensitive to 'seekers.' We've given up some parts of our old worship service, added screens, projectors, a sound system and a band. But the biggest change has been in our priorities, We 'old timers' are trying to think first of ways we can show Christ's face to people who are intimidated by the idea of church, or who were burned by the church. We used to think first about ourselves and what we liked. God is changing us as much as any of the people he is sending us."

As you sense from Sally's description, two main types of barriers prevent us from doing evangelism: barriers inside people's heads, and barriers in the church. Both can block people out. Let's look at the personal issues first.

> There *is* great news: God is in the business of healing us and our churches; Christ will stand at our elbow and point out our entrenched positions, our towering battlements and those legions of yeomen who are always retipping arrows and heating oil. The Spirit can lead us to drain moats, open drawbridges, and build wheelchair-accessible bridges! We slam the door shut on the Gospel, but Christ opens windows in lives and in churches.

Individuals' Barriers and Bridges

Almost every one of us has blocks about sharing our faith. We have internal medieval castles, complete with moats! Many of us are embarrassed or feel as if we don't know how to talk about our spiritual lives or our churches. Obviously, ideas and feelings affect our priorities and our actions. If we don't feel comfortable talking about our faith, we're not likely to do it!

We discovered three primary personal barriers to doing evangelism:

1. The most solid barrier to evangelism, the anti-evangelistic bedrock upon which we build our churches, is that most pastors and laypeople in mainline churches are not clear *why* to do

evangelism. If we don't know _**why**_ to do evangelism, we'll never get to the question of _**how**_ to do it (chapter 1).

2. Once people recognize the importance of evangelism, we discovered that a typical fear about faith sharing kicks in, even among pastors who are leading great evangelistic congregations! It's usually expressed as, "I don't want to risk a friendship," or, "I don't want to pressure people."[2]

3. A third common barrier, and a fairly easy one to deal with, is, "I don't know **how** to talk about my faith."[3]

Individual Barriers to Faith Sharing

1. I don't know why to do evangelism.
2. I don't want to risk a friendship.
3. I don't know how to talk about my faith.

**Dismantling the barriers:** The great news is that the act of identifying barriers helps us build bridges. If we know why to do evangelism, we'll start being motivated to share our faith. We'll begin seeing opportunities. If we identify our fears about sharing our faith, our fears of risking friendships, our fears of not knowing what to say, then we can talk with other Christians about it. At that point, we usually realize that every one of us has bits of hesitation. Then we can learn and practice helpful ways of talking about our faith. Now we are not blocking the Spirit from using us. See the process? If we will be brave enough to see and dismantle our barriers, the process of talking about our fears and practicing with our friends becomes the means of developing new skills and confidence. We have used the stone and concrete of our old barriers for bridge construction!

The typical barrier for people raised in mainline congregations is that we are foggy on why it matters that anyone be Christian. Most mainline Christians have little fear of Hell, but a horror of being embarrassed or looking obnoxious! Dismantling the barriers for most mainline Christians involves serious thinking, talking and praying about our relationships with Christ. If we are going to share faith, we need to know why we think it matters that we, or anyone else, are Christian.

Many people whose faith was formed in more traditional evangelical or charismatic churches have trouble with evangelism because they felt pressured to do it. The thought of evangelism feels negative to them. A 50-year-old evangelical woman lawyer articulated this barrier beautifully, "I always felt I wasn't really a Christian if I didn't do evangelism—door knocking, inviting people to church activities. I was in a campus ministry…Your ministry success was unofficially based on how many baptisms you performed each year. Less than 100 was clearly not successful. It never occurred to me that evangelism was sharing something you enjoy with someone you like (like quilting or dog shows). It was something all Christians had to do to go to Heaven. So, as you can guess, it's a touchy subject for me."

The grace-filled idea that "evangelism [could be] sharing something you enjoy with someone you like" was barrier-dismantling for her. Our barriers often dissolve if we identify them, look at them, discuss them, and pray to see old situations with new eyes.

Un-muting the Mute Button

We discovered one big difference between successful evangelistic congregations and "typical" churches. Evangelistic churches, like many good churches, concentrate on helping people grow in their faith lives through spiritual practices. But the evangelistic churches also hone in, with laser-like focus, on helping their members articulate and share their growing faith. This focus on faith and on faith sharing is evident in sermons, in small groups and in congregational financial priorities.

We're smart people. If we know *why* to share our faith (for example, that Christianity is true, or that being a Christian makes our life better in specific ways), we will be able to talk about it. Congregations with evangelistic faith encourage members to invite friends to church. They train people to recognize and articulate their faith. Training to share faith can happen from any theological perspective, but it always involves helping people identify (a) the pathway of their individual walks with Christ, (b) how God is active in their lives, (c) the power of the church community and (d) how to talk about these things in normal words.

People who share their faith say that it's hard because it is so personal. Practice with church friends first helps. Trying little steps like inviting someone to worship or to an event at church helps. And yet, with support of others from church as we saw in chapter 5, once you try talking about the depths of faith with others, it is exciting. Talking about God and what you are learning spiritually is actually one of the ways your own faith will grow and deepen.

Did you ever help a friend who didn't understand a class study for the exam? The first time I did it, I remember feeling frustrated because I was sure being nice to a friend was going to waste my precious study time. The exact opposite happened. When I struggled to explain hard material, simply and clearly, to my clueless friend, I understood it better myself. The structure of what I was learning, the most important points, fell into place in my own head. This is probably why teachers love teaching. You understand anything better when you

> The grace-filled idea that evangelism could be "sharing something you enjoy with someone you like" was barrier-dismantling for her.

try to put it into words. Could that be one reason why Christ asks us to help spread the Gospel to the ends of the earth? Did he want us to begin to get it ourselves by explaining it to others?

There's a great line in the movie *Jerry Maguire*.[4] Tom Cruise was a sports agent trying to help a frustrating, pig-headed, egotistical football player (whom Cruise really liked). In one scene, Tom Cruise said one line about 15 different ways to try to get it into the tight end's head, "Help *me* help you." "Help me help *you*!" "*HELP* me *HELP* you!" Maybe that's why Jesus asks us to help with evangelism. It's a cosmic "Help me help *you*" from God!

Okay, so we *can* learn to talk about our faith, if for no other reason than to help God help us! The important thing about our personal barriers to faith sharing is to: (1) identify them, (2) talk about them, (3) do something to dismantle them. Now let's think about the barriers and bridges we find in churches.

Your Church's Barriers and Bridges

Think! What does your church feel like to first-time visitors and new members? The Lincoln Memorial or the medieval fortress? Something in between? What's your best guess? A church's biggest barrier is that long-term members can't see their churches with fresh eyes. When you ask church members to describe their congregation, the two most common descriptions are: "Our church is so *friendly*." and "We're like a family." These statements couldn't be more true. The problem is that we forget what families are like!

Church is like family. Have you been a stranger at someone else's family reunion? Have you ever been the brand new son-in-law? There's everybody, laughing and joking, grabbing the good kind of baked beans and knowing to avoid Aunt Letty's sponge cake. They all know who's nice, who's fun and who's a big pain. They know the jokes. They know Uncle Larry drinks too much and that then, if you're a woman, you'd better give him Wide Berth. They all know not to pay attention to Aunt Edna, who manages to say something nasty to anyone within earshot. We all know *our* families; they're normal. It's *other* people's families that are nuts! But some families work hard to help new people fit in and to feel welcome. Other families make you earn your place at the table!

Churches are the same way. Once you're inside and have your group of friends and your round of activities, you forget about the first impressions and the initiations rites. You don't even **see** the nasty sponge cake or Uncle Larry's encroachments upon ladies' nether limbs. Aunt Edna's mouth may move, but you don't hear

Evangelistic churches concentrate on helping people grow in their faith lives through spiritual practices. These churches hone in, with laser-like focus, on helping their members articulate and share their growing faith.

sound coming out any more. Once you're in the family and have your allies and buddies, once you've spent a couple of Thanksgivings and Christmases together, it's friendly. It's family. And that's how you describe it. It's just like your church. It's a family.

First-time visitors. It's almost impossible to see our own churches with a fresh eye. Can you imagine what it would be like to be a first-time visitor? Think about a first visit from beginning to end. If you were new in town, how would you learn about the existence of the church? Worship times? Get the yellow pages and look up the ad. Drive by your church, pretending you don't know it's there. What does it look like? Can you read the sign?

Call the church phone. How's the phone answering machine message? Does it give directions and worship times? Is the secretary friendly? Pretend you're a fly on the wall this Sunday. Watch and see how any visitors are greeted. Look at their expressions. Are they lost? Looking intimidated? Do people talk with them and invite them into their pew? Are close parking spots and back pews available two minutes before the service starts, the time when visitors often arrive? Are bathrooms and coat racks clearly labeled? Is the building entrance accessible? Well-kept? **IS THE NURSERY SPOTLESS? and Easy to Find?** How many people talk with new visitors? Show them around? Invite them for lunch afterwards?

Many fears accompany first-time visitors (remember chapter 4). How are you working to calm those fears? Do you have social events to which your members can invite visitors? One congregation has an annual women's Christmas lunch. Two members set a table for eight of their unchurched friends with their most beautiful china and silver and flowers from home. They invite their friends, act as hostesses and have a program on a faith theme. People with no connection to a church may be scared of going to a worship service, but it's rare to find someone scared of lunch!

Is your worship service inspiring and meaningful? Is it over-whelming or tedious? Do the music and language feel comfortable or foreign to the bandwidth of people God is calling you to reach? Do you spell out the Lord's prayer and when to stand or sit? Many churches print the words worshipers say or sing in the bulletin or on projection screens. We can no longer count on people knowing the structure of a worship service, the doxology or even the Lord's prayer. Is there welcoming follow-up (a gift, a call, an invitation, a visit)? It is such a challenge to think about first impressions!

Returning visitors. Next comes another set of questions. How easy it is for second- or third-time visitors to find a place or small

Most mainline Christians have little fear of Hell, but a horror of being embarrassed or looking obnoxious!

group in the church so that they make real friends in the congregation? How many opportunities do they have to learn more about the faith? To have opportunities to serve others?

After joining. Think further down the road. How easy is it for new members to ease into positions of leadership and responsibility? Do you support new leaders and train them, or ask them to do a job and let them figure it out on their own? Does it take a decade to be welcomed into central places of service and commitment?

Feedback. Think about these things yourselves. Then check out your thinking. Give feedback cards to all visitors. Provide feedback cards in each pew. People will write things they would ***never*** have the courage to say to your face. Always remember the key point—***ask the people who know.*** You can ask the elders how well you're doing with first impressions, or the ease of integration of new members into the congregation's life. They will have a few good ideas. But if we want to know for real, we have to ask the visitors and the new members themselves! It's like the family reunion. The new son-in-law will have insights now that he'll have forgotten in three years. After three years, he ***still*** knows more about what it's like to be new in the family than the grandmother knows.

> We understand anything better when we try to say it out loud. Could this be one reason Christ asks us to share our faith? Is the Great Commission (Mt. 28:18–20) a cosmic "Help me help *you*" from God?

Many books and many articles on the Internet can give you wonderful ideas to try in your church. Once you begin to see the barriers you have up, as individuals and as a church, you can begin to take steps to dismantle them. Like Sally's congregation, ask the Spirit to help you see where you're stuck in old habits or how you could be more open. Ask for help from a consultant, from a denominational minister, from visitors, or from pastors and laypeople from churches that are doing a good job of evangelism.

Bridges can be built, bit by bit. Those first forays toward faith sharing often feel like swinging over quicksand on a Tarzan rope. They have none of the secure sense of standing on the bedrock of habit! But don't worry! Soon, with many people helping, you could be tiptoeing gingerly on a sturdy rope ladder over a waterfall. Next you'll be rambling across a covered bridge. One day you may open the door of your church and see the Golden Gate Bridge leading straight into your sanctuary.

DISCUSSION QUESTIONS

1. How is your individual prayer going? Spend the first 10-20 minutes of your time together sharing the highlights of your prayer time with each other. How have you seen God this week?

2. Did any Bible passage come to mind when you read this chapter? Does one occur to you now? Discuss how it connects with what you have read. (If no passages come to mind, you might want to look at: Hebrews 13:1–3; Colossians 4:3–4; Colossians 3:12–17.)

3. Have you ever tried to share your faith? What happened? What felt right in the experience? What might you do differently next time? Does anything stop you from talking with others about faith? What could help change that?

4. Think about the bandwidths of evangelism. Who is your church already reaching? Discuss what God is doing to connect people with your church now. What would be the logical next step to expand your church's evangelism? Do you have any inklings, any promptings from the Spirit about whom you might be called to reach? Does the "logical next step" you identified fit with the way the promptings of the Spirit feel? Talk about *that*!

5. Is your church like the Lincoln Memorial for visitors and new members, with its wide, easy entrance steps? Or is it like a medieval castle complete with turrets and moat? Name any barriers to visitors or new members that you can think of. What are the top three barriers you would dismantle? How do the barriers change when you switch stations to a different bandwidth? Are these barriers different, depending on which bandwidth of evangelism you're tuned to? Which are the first three bridges you'd build if you could wave a magic wand?

6. So what are you going to do?

At the beginning of each session:

A. Light a candle to remind us of Christ's presence;

B. Repeat aloud, together: "**We agree that we will hold everything shared in this group in complete confidence.**"

EXERCISE

Divide into groups of three or four. Sit quietly with a notebook and pen in your lap. Pray in silence for a couple of minutes. Ask God to show you what you need to know about what your church looks like/feels like to people who have:

1. never heard of it
2. never been inside
3. not joined a small group yet
4. not been members long
5. never served as board chair

Take notes as words, images or ideas occur to you.

The leader will close the silent time with a prayer. Open your eyes. Divide into small groups. Let each group make a large drawing of your church on newsprint. Label the barriers and bridges you thought about during the prayer time, or that occur to you as you talk. Pay particular attention to the insights of people who have not been in your church long. You are an evangelistic architect. What would you do to redesign this "building"?

As a full group, talk about the small groups' drawings and see if the groups came up with similar barriers and bridges. What are possible next steps? Pray in silence for two or three minutes and ask Christ to show you what one or two changes he would like you to make. Talk about it.

Exercise during the week: Now it's time to test out your perceptions. Half of you invite a new member out to lunch and ask him or her about the church. What does the person perceive as the welcoming strengths of the church? Its barriers to newcomers? What works beautifully? What could the church do better?

The other half of your group could each ask a good friend to visit your church and pretend to be shy. Invite someone you know will be able to be honest with you. Ask these friends to call the church to get worship times and directions. Give them the Church Visitor Questionnaire (a hospitality inventory) that you'll find at www.GraceNet.info/more_resources.aspx. Ask them to keep track of how many people spoke with them, what was welcoming, what was offputting. Would they come back? What could you do better? Don't forget to thank them exuberantly and to invite them back for real! If you make changes later based on their help, let them know about it. (And ask them to visit again!)

---

[1]We do not have exact statistics for these categories. The Mainline Evangelism Project did collect recent statistics on adult baptisms, which help us measure how churches are doing in evangelism with unchurched people—Bandwidths 101.8 and 101.9. What we know for sure is that only half of 1% of 30,000 congregations performed what we considered a significant number of adult baptisms (see introduction). Compare that to the fact that almost all of those 30,000 congregations would be working in some way to help their young people have a relationship with Christ.

[2]The Mainline Evangelism Project survey showed that there are inner barriers to evangelism even in pastors and members of churches who are doing some of the most effective evangelism with unchurched adults in the country: 38.3% of these pastors report that they have hesitations because they don't want to risk a friendship, 70.8% of the pastors don't want to pressure others. Meanwhile, 39.5% of laypeople don't want to risk a friendship, 83.5% don't want to pressure others. Yet, they have figured out ways to acknowledge their hesitations and do evangelism anyway!

[3]An overwhelming majority of 73.3% of laity say that not knowing how to talk about their faith is a great barrier to doing evangelism. Meanwhile, 24.5% of pastors and evangelism leaders cite this as somewhat of a barrier or a great barrier. Finally, 19.3% of pastors/leaders and 63.8% of laity say that not knowing how to talk about their faith is at least somewhat a barrier. All the statistics in endnotes 1 through 3

are from the great evangelistic churches whose baptisms of uchurched adults placed them in the top half of 1%! Be encouraged!

[4]*Jerry Maguire,* Sony Pictures, 1996.

CHAPTER 6

Smart Sailing

Navigating Distractions, Getting Started

Imagine floating on a big raft in the lake. The sun is warm. Close your eyes. Feel the drift and swell of little waves. Life is easy. Life is good. If you fall asleep and bump into the edge of the dock, it's just a little jolt as you float lazily in the sun.

Were you ever a 12-year-old at the lake? Did you hitch up a sail to that old raft? In a decent breeze, you could really get that thing going. "Alright, ye swabs, haul in those sheets and belay the mizzenmast!" (or is it "take a belaying pin to those scurvy blackguards on the f'oc's'l"?); well, "hand me me grog." *Ahhhhhrrrrrrrrr, Pirrrrattes*. The thing is, when a pirate raft gets going, if the breeze is good and if the cap'n is 12 and paying more attention to the mutinous knaves aboard than to the rudder, you can take that dock at quite a clip…with impressive effect upon both ship and crew. The dock's usually fine.

It's the same with churches. Most of our congregations are floating along, drifting luxuriously in the warm sun, drowsy with the gentle rise and fall of the waves. Life is easy. Life is good. So long as no hotshots in motorboats cut too close, we're fine. But every once in a while somebody gets the idea to hitch up a sail and try to catch the Spirit. Then the old ship starts to move. Sails billow in gusting winds; the ship is heeling, spray flying; life is joyous, alive, free. And dangerous.

Did you know that one of the most ancient pictures of the church was a ship? It's drawn in the Roman Catacombs and in our earliest Christian art. As in the gospel of John, the Spirit is the wind, moving the church through dangerous waters.

A decision to let God use us to share real faith pries us loose from old habits, perceptions and moorings. We always thought of our church as First Church, on the corner of Broadway and Main Streets. Now First Church is a clipper ship, canvas spread, filled with treasures, bound for the Indies. You may feel a little seasick. Change is hard. God is trustworthy.

I began ministry like a 12-year-old pirate, hoisting a sail on the raft, whooping, "Whoa, this is so ***cool!***" We got going at quite a clip. The dear old raft could have hit that dock hard or wound up on rocks. Thank heavens some great sailors were in the boat. Captains of frigates, the admiral on his flagship, radioed instructions in response to my S.O.S. signals. I didn't have a clue about the type of ministry I had slipped into by hoisting that sail. Sometimes I felt scared. Other times I was blissfully ignorant of skimming past underwater rocks. Experienced sailors read rocks by wave patterns. I was looking at the sunrise and the flying fish. That church did well only by the grace of God, not by Martha Grace.

After hearing similar stories from other pastors, it's clear to me I wasn't alone in my blithe, sailing ignorance. Everyone who has tried to put a sail on a raft has had their shuddering-into-the-dock moments! Some of what I'll say here may sound simple. I will be grateful if it gives you one or two thoughts that help you watch more closely, see rocks earlier, or sail through shoals.

> Christ is the calmer of waves, the master of the storm. God holds the untamable chaos of our lives in God's hands and can calm it. Don't stop. Keep going. Step up communication with your team members. Step up communication with God. Your instinct will be that this slows the pace. Your instinct is probably wrong.

The key point is that life with the Spirit, or a decision to let God use us to share real faith, pries us loose from old habits, perceptions and moorings. We always thought of our church as First Church, on the corner of Broadway and Main Streets. Now First Church is a clipper ship, canvas spread, filled with treasures, bound for the Indies. You may feel a little seasick. Change is hard. God is trustworthy.

Waves and Weather Conditions Changing Churches Meet

If you take one point from this chapter, let it be this: safety lies in God, not in our habits. If you feel unsafe, talk with each other and pray. Hand God your feelings, and ask what you should do next. Do that individually and together. Our safety always lies in God, as dangerous-feeling, seasick-swirling, lee-shore-looming as life with God may feel! Our safety, as well as our joy, lies in our glimpses of the Lord, in letting the Spirit play through our sails and move us forward. When wild stuff happens, don't panic. Talk with each other, run it past someone wise, and pray.

Let's examine sample wave and weather conditions many evangelistic churches meet.

1. Growing pains ("outer" waves)

2. Conflict ("inner" waves)

3. Distractions

1. Growing Pains ("Outer" Waves)

Growing pains are the natural result of change. Children can grow so quickly that they have pain in their joints. Wrists shoot out of sleeves, ankles extrude from pants that were let down last week. It's exhausting to watch! Churches can be the same way.

Example: Granville Church began praying. Faith deepened. Members felt a call to share their blossoming faith with others. Within three years, the church grew from 110 adults in worship to 215. Sixty children and youth worship with them instead of eight. Granville has hired a young associate pastor. Worship is exciting. The senior pastor is working 80 hours a week to keep up with the new people and to orient the associate and a second church secretary.

Old ways of doing things aren't working in this changing environment. Growth requires new software, a new Web site, new accounting and record-keeping systems, new ways of integrating members and training teachers. Some of these learning curves are steep! The church has only four classrooms for 28 small groups. Three groups need the one big common space at the same time. The sanctuary is 90% full. A second service is in the works. For now, last-minute visitors have trouble parking and finding seats.

Diagnosis: Waves are beginning to roll around Granville. The wind has picked up. I call these "outer" waves because most people can see that the upsets are the result of the objective situation of the church growing. Most members don't feel as if other people are causing the frustrations. They see that it's the situation. People's feelings don't tend to get hurt. Members fumbling thorough new systems of reserving a classroom may feel frustrated, but not mad. Their instinct is to laugh or shrug, rather than swear or go tell a friend about what just happened.

Granville's situation becomes dangerous if they ignore the stresses of change. Leaders can lighten loads and change pacing in churches. One thing is sure: pastors cannot work 80-hour weeks for long without damage to their spiritual lives, families, health or abilities to perceive situations and deal with them in the Spirit. I predict that if Granville's pastor doesn't attend to his spiritual, psychological, physical and family health, by the end of this fourth year, he will be emotionally brittle and making "people" mistakes. He is probably making them now. The same holds true of every leader in the church. We can all put on a big push in a good cause, but an adrenaline rush that lasts for years corrodes physical and spiritual health.

Sailing Conditions

1. Growing pains ("outer" waves)
2. Conflict ("inner" waves)
3. Distractions

See the situation early. The key to dealing with outer waves is to see them coming so you can make adjustments. Spot those "outer waves" early and talk about them. Who will see these types of waves first and most accurately? Individuals who are sensitive to people and to what's happening in the church. Ask the assistant in charge of scheduling or the pastor's spouse. Ask the quiet, wise deacon who prays and is in the church office a lot. These people can tell you things others don't see. They usually will not volunteer the information.

Don't count on the people leading the change to monitor the pacing accurately. Leaders tend to speed up under pressure and think they can handle "one more thing." They lose perspective as they lose sleep and get into addictive patterns of coping. Ask them what's going on, but know that you'll probably get more accurate perceptions from their spouses!

Don't count on the people who are upset by changes to see whether the church is moving too quickly. Some people have very faithful and constant personalities. They are often wonderful with seeing the details of situations. They are the salt of the earth. But they have a hard time making changes. Some people can make adjustments in other areas of their lives, but need the church to stay put at Main and Broadway. Switching classrooms can rattle these people for months. Sometimes those switches have to be made, even though it is hard on some people. Understanding and tact in making changes go a long way in helping folks adapt, but their feelings shouldn't be used to plan the church's pace of change.

Who can help? You can do very specific, practical things to deal with growing pains—the outer waves. Ask someone outside the church to help you monitor and deal with the changes you are navigating. It is best to ask someone to help you early on—before the wind picks up and the waves get choppy. Your pastor can work with a "coach." Your denominational pastor can advise you. Other churches that have navigated growth and change can help, give advice, encourage you! Sometimes large congregations host great conferences to help others learn from their successes and mistakes. The presentations can be very helpful. You may meet another participant who gives you the exact insight or piece of encouragement you need.

God is there to help. God will not lead you out of Egypt, into the desert and dump you there. You are God's messengers. You're trying to serve God. You are not alone. Pray by yourself. Jesus loves you and will spend time with you. He will care for your soul, body and family. Pray with others in the church. The Spirit will help you when

One of the hardest things about change in churches is that people think of church as the one fixed point in an otherwise spinning universe. Our relationships with God have to be Mother Teresa-mature before we see God as our stability—our North Star—instead of the church. God is the North Star, the fixed point by which we can navigate while the church sails, while the world swirls and buffets us.

you don't even know how to pray. The Spirit will give you glimmers of understanding and subtle leadings for where to turn next.

Christ is the calmer of waves, the master of the storm. God holds the untamable chaos of our lives in God's hands and can calm it. Don't stop. Keep going. Step up communication with your team members. Step up communication with God. Your instinct will be that this slows the pace. Your instinct is probably wrong. Talk, pray, attend to your judicatory people, your coaches. Don't do everything yourself. Ask for help. Don't panic. Sail smart. You are, now and forever, in God's hands.

2. Conflict ("Inner" Waves)

God is our North Star. The church is the moving ship. Remember, growing churches are changing. After a while, we will have to sacrifice things we love to help new people move into faith. We all have different tolerances for change, but it is hard for each of us to let go of dear old things we love. In some ways, our lives are a continual process of surrendering the old and adjusting to the new. Sometimes we make a natural transition (we graduate from fourth grade and move into fifth). Sometimes a change is exciting and wonderful (we get married). Sometimes a change is traumatic or dreaded (an accident or a death). But we consistently face something new.

God is always in the new place.

One of the hardest things about change in churches is that people think of church as the one fixed point in an otherwise spinning universe. Our relationships with God have to be Mother Teresa–mature before we see God as our stability—our North Star—instead of the church. The reality is that God *is* the North Star, the fixed point by which we can navigate while the church sails, while the world swirls and buffets us.

Most of us, most of the time, only see God through a particular chapel window, from the viewpoint of the end of the fourth pew on the left, through the lens of a particular pastor's sermons. We live in the particulars of our lives. Because God and church are so important to us, any fussing with those particulars can threaten us.

A decision to follow the leadings of the Spirit and enter into intentional evangelism will bring slightly different responses from everyone in your church. Some will whoop with excitement as they clamber up the rigging. Others will be seasick. Some will feel as if they have been impressed (kidnapped from a seaside tavern, waking up aboard a ship heading out on a three-year tour of the South Seas).

The best way is to help each other navigate the change and look for God, our North Star, in each new place our church sails. God will always be with us, but we can get scared, shut our eyes and forget to look. The result can be conflict, or "inner" waves.

We must be gentle with each other. We each have a different focus, a different tolerance for change.

The best way is to help each other navigate the change and look for God, our North Star, in each new place our church sails. God will always be with us, but we can get scared, shut our eyes and forget to look. The result can be conflict, or "inner" waves.

Example: Rocky Springs Church shows us the same situation as Granville Church, but with these additional elements: Rocky Springs has experienced the same type of growth, but the pastor is running on empty. One Sunday school class and some of the elders are upset over the children's program using their space. Exterminators just sprayed the Senior High School room for roaches because the kids keep grinding Doritos™ and chocolate chip cookies into the carpet. People are grumpy. The pastor's daughter's impressive ship tattoo is causing significant talk. ("And why do they let her wear her jeans that low ***anyway***?") Board members leave meetings with headaches. Long-term members mutter about "the new people." The elder who caused so much trouble for the last two pastors is winding up and starting to make phone calls. Groups are forming. Stomachs are nervous. Teeth are on edge.

Diagnosis: Growing pains or conflict? Do you see the difference between "outer" waves (simple growing pains), and these "inner" waves (conflict)? Growing pains are about "things," a situation. Conflict feels different. Some people are angry. Some are avoidant. Some have hurt feelings. Some are suspicious and taking sides. The church's forward movement is starting to bog down. Water is sloshing into the hold. The difference between growing pains and conflict is like the phrase from the guy in *The Godfather* who just shot someone's father: "Look, kid, this isn't personal. It's business."[1] Growing pains aren't personal. They're business. Conflict feels very, very personal.

Identify conflict early. Just as with growing pains, the earlier you see and start to deal with conflict, the more easily it can be resolved. Here are some ways of seeing the situation quickly, before it progresses too far:

> ■ ***Listen to your sensitive people.*** Who are they? Your intercessors, key leaders, pastors' spouses, spiritually mature elders tend to be good candidates. People with strong leadership gifts, the driving initiators of change, usually do not see conflict early. (One of these great leaders told me, "No, *I* don't feel stress. I'm a carrier!")

Be open to mid-course corrections. Leading a congregation, like sailing, calls for tiny adjustments of sails and pinpoint responsiveness to new conditions. Just keep the ship pointed in the same direction.

■ *Canaries in the mineshaft.* Have you heard stories of the old days of coal mining when miners took canaries down into the mineshaft with them? Then, if they cut into a pocket of poisonous gas, the canaries would be affected first. A canary drooping on its perch was the miners' first warning of trouble. Some people are like those canaries. They sense the first whiff of conflict, recognize what's going on, and can articulate it clearly. Others can be quite unconscious about why they're edgy. (These are often great people you love.) These "canaries" go off like bottle rockets in meetings, snap out some nasty comment on the way out of worship, launch into a tirade over a spoon filed away in the wrong drawer. They are your canaries in the mineshaft. They are more sensitive than most to the gasses of conflict. *What* they're saying is probably exaggerated. *The fact* that they're exploding is what matters. The explosions themselves constitute your early warning system. Thank them! Pay attention! Those canaries are singing an important song.

> The difference between growing pains and conflict is like the phrase from the guy in *The Godfather* who just shot someone's father: "Look, kid, this isn't personal. It's business." Growing pains aren't personal. They're business. Conflict feels ***personal.***

Disagreements can be healthy. Conflict can reach dangerous levels. As in good marriages and close friendships, churches engaged in vibrant ministry always have differences of opinion and some friction. Differences and a certain degree of friction are part of human relationships. Without some change and some challenge, relationships and churches stagnate. Their souls grow numb. They die of boredom.

However, at some point differences and friction can move to a level of destructive conflict. The Rocky Springs Church is starting down this path. Their mild to middling conflict could escalate to the point where it tears down ministries and leaves streams of wounded people in its wake. The healthiest way of dealing with differences of opinion and friction is to listen carefully, talk kindly and honestly, get some outside help, and pray together.

Be open to mid-course corrections. Flexibility counts at this point! Pay attention to your advisors, your coach, your denominational ministers. Sometimes the sails need to be let out a little bit. Let the ship slow down a trifle while people adjust to the new movement. Leading a congregation, like sailing, asks for tiny adjustments of sails and pinpoint responsiveness to new conditions. Just keep the ship pointed in the same direction.

Antagonists. Most conflict in churches is the result of normal people reacting to extraordinary situations. Sometimes, however, conflict is due to people who thrive on conflict and chaos, who willfully attack others. Kenneth Haugk, founder of Stephen Ministries, calls them *antagonists* and describes them as: "individuals who, on the basis of non-substantive evidence, go out of their way to make insatiable demands, usually attacking the person or performance of others. These attacks are selfish in nature, tearing down rather than building up, and are frequently directed against those in a leadership capacity."[2] The Rocky Springs elder who has a history of difficulties with pastors and is currently making phone calls and stirring up trouble might well be an antagonist. Churches are peculiarly vulnerable to antagonists because most people, from church leaders to members in the pews, are trying to live together kindly and lovingly. A person who launches a blatant, destructive attack baffles us. We don't intuitively know how to respond with firm enough boundaries. Dr. Haugk's book gives clear, practical, specific suggestions for recognizing and dealing with people who stir up destructive, unhealthy conflict.

Who can help with conflict? The same people and resources who can help with growing pains/outer waves: coaches, denominational ministers, conferences, great books, colleagues and God. Everything said in the growing pains section applies here, but it is particularly important to ask an outside person to help you navigate through conflict. It's hard to see and trust each other fully once feelings are riled up. When a situation has gotten to be "personal, not business," none of our perceptions are completely accurate. We see through the haze of our own emotions. An independent outsider can help us navigate the situation.

Summary: It is normal for churches to experience some degree of discord if they are growing. Some conflict is part of creativity and change. But conflict can move to destructive levels. If your church is experiencing conflict,

a. identify it early;
b. work with your outside advisors;
c. ask God for healing, protection and leadings of the Spirit;
d. be open to mid-course corrections and changes of pace;
e. remember that the call to share the Gospel is Christ's. Keep going.

Do you remember the end of the movie *Star Wars*?[3] The hero, Luke Skywalker, is leading a small band of heroic pilots into the world-destroying Death Star. If they can shoot a bomb into a narrow shaft that leads to the core of the Death Star, they can destroy it. Bad guys

---

Keep an eagle eye on the weather. You're safer if you spot situations quickly!

are shooting at them. Good guys are catching on fire and exploding. It's terrifying. It's hard to concentrate on the pinpoint precision shot they're trying to make at such speed, in so much confusion. The voice you hear through the scene says, "Stay on target…stay on target."

That's what we need to do in conflict. Stay on target.

3. Distractions

John Peterman, founder and president of the brilliantly quirky retail company (www.jpeterman.com) once told me that organizations are like rubber bands. You can stretch them, and they adapt. You keep stretching, they keep getting longer. But if you stretch too quickly, or too far, the rubber band flips out of your fingers and snaps back to its original size.

This is a dynamic of institutional change that applies to churches. We stretch the rubber band until we get to a point of having a new, larger, rubber band to put in its place. Then we can stretch the new rubber band and retire the old one. In churches, you stretch the rubber band as the sanctuary begins to fill to overflowing. The new worship service you put in place is like a new rubber band. It's flexible and stretches. It relieves the pressure, and you can fill it (stretch the new rubber band) again. At times when a church is changing, the rubber band is stretched thin. The Granville Church is stretching. The Rocky Springs Church is in danger of snapping back.

Stretched people and churches are vulnerable to distractions. The further the rubber band is stretched, the more vulnerable. I don't want to give just one scenario here, as in Rocky Springs and Granville. There isn't just one scenario for distractions. Distractions can look like anything, wear any kind of clothes. However, the hallmark of a distraction is that it tends to drag your attention away from your focus. Let's look at some typical distractions, so that you begin to see the patterns.

> Distractions can look like anything, wear any kind of clothes. The hallmark of a distraction is that it tends to drag our attention away from our focus.

Other Good Things

Can you hear the voices in the board meeting? "Let's have everybody take a course in Christian money management this year." "Let's start a ministry to children in the neighborhood." "But we're *helping* people with the thrift shop." Which do you do? All of them? Any of them?

The frustration with following a charted course in a church is that churches can do *many* important ministries. If we try to decide to do a ministry based on whether it is a *good* ministry, we can start to drift off God's course or end up on rocks. Most ministries are important. How do we decide what to do?

We have to discern which ministries to do based on what God is calling **us, specifically,** to do. If God has called your church, and you as a person, to found a homeless shelter, you **must** do it! If God wants you to lobby in the state legislature for environmental issues, **that's** your job. If God asks you to do evangelism, **that's** your call. Stay on target.

Once you know your call, you can make decisions about which ministries to do. The question is: Will this ministry support the call? If you have five ideas of ministries that would support the call, you look at them, pray about them with your ministry team. Discuss and discern together which one or which combination of ideas best fit your gifts, situation, your time and money and the people you're called to serve.

God is the one with perspective, the only coach who can call this play. We need to try to be flexible. God can change plans. Situations change. But stay on target. Follow your call. Ask first: "What is our call?" Ask second: "Will this ministry serve our call? Is this the way God is calling us to spend our limited time and limited resources?" That is the framework with which to make decisions. Remember: the "Don't Go There" list and the "Stop Doing" list are as important as the "To Do" list!

Alluring Distractions

A banker friend described giving a major presentation at the bank's annual board meeting. They were running late. It was past time for lunch. Down the table, one of the board members pulled a Hershey™ bar with almonds out of her purse and slipped a bite into her mouth. Herb, my friend, said, "What was the deal? Okay, I was sort of hungry, but I was **captivated** by the thought of that candy bar. The almonds were calling to me. I must have been staring at that chocolate like a lost soul. I bumbled a sentence, then lost the thread of my argument. I felt as if I ought to stop my talk, sit down, take a sip of my coffee and say, "Hi, I'm Herb. I'm a chocoholic.'"

Is there anything in your life so alluring it makes you fumble your presentation?

Oh, these alluring distractions are brutal! They can be **anything**, although food, praise and recognition, an attraction to a person, television, checking your e-mail constantly, Internet sexual searches, spending money, living through children and drinking too much are

> If we try to decide to do a ministry based on whether it is a good ministry, we can start to drift off God's course or end up on rocks. Most ministries are important. How do we decide what to do? We have to discern which ministries to do based on what God is calling us, specifically, to do.

top contenders! An alluring distraction distorts, captivates, ensorcells. It pulls us away from our focus on God and the Spirit's promptings.

How can you tell if you are dealing with an alluring distraction? Perhaps the best clue is if you feel like tucking it away out of other people's sight. If you feel like hiding something you're doing or thinking, *tell* someone about it. If you feel hesitant to be open with some trusted person, you may be dealing with an alluring distraction. What do you do then? Tell someone about it!! Light and air work wonders on anaerobic infections and alluring distractions.

The further the rubber band is stretched, the more vulnerable we can be to this type of distraction. A fascinating person, a mind-numbing book, a bag of Oreos™ start to shimmer like a mirage in the desert when we're tired, emotionally isolated, stretched too thin, or not in good spiritual shape. Alluring distractions can act as canaries in the mineshaft! They show us when we're stretched too thin and need to take better care of ourselves. The best ways of coping are to talk with someone you trust; pray; get some sleep; go for a walk; play with the dog; work with a counselor, your accountability group or a 12-step group.

Do you see the effect of an alluring distraction? It's just like any other distraction. Its tendency is to deflect your attention from what God is calling you to do. What do you do about it? Drag your eyes away from the Hershey™ bar *and* the almonds. Fix the fumbled sentence. Finish your presentation. Stay on target!

Tragic Distractions

One of the sweetest-spirited pastors with whom I spoke in the Mainline Evangelism Project was a young pastor of a new church. He and the founding members prayed that God would send them people to love who were really different from them. God sent them a couple of bikers who were on drugs and dealing with arrests and prison. That presented a challenge!

But this remarkable group of people rose to the occasion. Those first "different" people have transformed lives today. They are drug-free, have brought many friends to the church and are now congregational leaders. About 850 people worshiped together only eight years after the church began. At the end of the eighth year, the wife of the associate pastor, a social worker who was part of the ministry team from the beginning, was killed in a car accident. The driver at fault was a stranger to the church. He was on drugs.

This is agonizing irony.

How can you tell if you are dealing with an alluring distraction? Perhaps the best clue is if you feel like tucking it away out of other people's sight. If you feel like hiding something you're doing or thinking, tell someone about it!

After a tragedy of this sort, the church must care for its soul, deal with its grief. The distraction in a situation like this would be if the pastor and key leaders started muttering, "Stay on Target…Stay on Target…Stay on Target," like a mantra. At a time like this, frantic recitation of "stay on target" can act as a defense against dealing with the leaders' own feelings. Leaders would be falling for the distraction if they tried to get the shell-shocked congregation psyched up for some cheery new outreach program.

A tragedy shatters the target. But beneath the evangelism target you saw before is ***another*** evangelism target, a deeper one you can't see yet.

A tragedy shatters the target.

But beneath the evangelism target you saw before is ***another*** target, a deeper one.

The point of evangelism is sharing the life with God you know. A tragedy opens up the possibility of a much deeper life with God. Whatever we learn, we can share with others later. What new things about faith can you learn during a time of tragedy? Tragedy gives us a glimpse of how fragile and precious life can be. It presents Job-like questions: "How could a loving God let such evil happen?" "What possible meaning could such tragedy have?" "Why did this happen to us, now, when we're working so hard and things are going so well?" "This isn't *fair*!"

It is frightening even to *think* these questions, let alone say them to another person or whisper them in God's direction. But asking these questions is the beginning of a new layer of spiritual growth. The more we can ask the questions—of the Bible, of our theologians, of each other, of God—the better. It also helps to allow ourselves to acknowledge some bit of our pain, our confusion, our anger. God is more real, more powerful, more loving than we ever know from easy times. We can learn this through tragedy, if we will.

If church members can hang in there with each other during the hard times, new growth will begin. It will be inner, soul growth. Don't worry about the evangelism target for this season. The target is the ***deeper*** evangelism target—to see life and people, yourself and Christ on the Cross, more clearly. God is alive and working throughout our most painful times. If we allow ourselves to feel the hardest feelings, ask the most painful questions, God will be able to reveal Godself to us in more powerful ways than before. You will know when it is time to share that even more profound good news. Soon, God will bring you new people who need *exactly* what you are learning now.

Confusing Distractions

Let's end this distractions talk on an easier note! Sometimes quirky distractions, "coincidental" distractions, can swirl up around us like a sudden sandstorm. The result is confusion, feeling rattled or off center. Like all the other distractions, confusing distractions tend to pull us away from a peaceful focus on Christ and our calls. Here are some examples:

Scenario A: It's Maundy Thursday. A tree falls on the power line, and the electricity goes out. The bulletins haven't been run. The church secretary receives a phone call from her child's school to let her know that she bounced a check for the first time in her life. She is mortified. The pastor is felled by a migraine.

Scenario B: Dense fog has socked the preacher for your Weekend Worship Extravaganza in at the Seattle-Tacoma Airport. The hospitality committee has forgotten the paper plates. They're frantic. As you leave the house to go meet with the group trying to figure out a new plan, your spouse asks sharply, "So, *why* did you let Johnny take your car when you knew you were going to be needing it? All right," in martyred tones, "you can use *my* car, but I wish you'd cleared it with me in advance." On your way to the meeting, you get a call that dear, 17-year-old, responsible Johnny had a fender bender in *your* new car. Aaaaaaahhhhhhhhhh!!!

Confusing distractions rattle us because they come in a rush and in a flurry. You could handle one thing, but at a critical moment, six odd, annoying little tests of your spiritual stability start swimming around you. As a pastor friend said, "I feel like I'm being minnowed to death." So, what do you do when you feel the nibbling begin?

Recognize what's going on. Knowing that you're dealing with a distraction gives you a handle on the situation. If you can, *say it out loud* to somebody, "Oh…, I think these are confusing distractions! I know this crazy feeling!" Then *pray* with someone. Ask God for peace and protection from getting rattled and off center. You might want to memorize Philippians 4:6–7 and use it as your prayer: "Do not worry about anything, but in everything by prayer and supplication with thanksgiving let your requests be made known to God. And the peace of God, which surpasses all understanding, will guard your hearts and your minds in Christ Jesus."

Confusion tends to drag us out of Christ's peace and into anxiety. We need to remind ourselves that we are in this situation because God has called us here. God will *never* desert us during a crazy time. If we train ourselves to turn to Christ and ask for help, distractions will dissolve.

Stay on target. Once we have recognized that we're just dealing with distractions, talked with a person or two, prayed for peace and protection against getting all frazzled, we can get on with it! We figure

How to Cope with Distractions

1. *Recognize it* as a distraction as quickly as you can.

2. *Name it* and get it out in the open with the people with whom you're in ministry.

3. *Pray* that God will take care of it, protect everyone and show you the path to tread through the difficulty.

4. *Stay on target.* Go to your board meeting or prayer retreat or meeting with your friend as planned.

out backup plans. The electricity may go back on. If not, somebody runs the bulletin copies somewhere else. We pray that the fog lifts in Seattle and arrange for a backup preacher. Once we're calmed down, the details aren't a problem.

Growing pains and conflict, distractions and difficulties will crop up whenever God entrusts us with work that matters. Growing pains will stretch us. Conflict can hook our emotions. Sometimes conflict will enrage or scare us. Distractions can confuse, entice, terrify. Some distractions are tragic, others merely unsettling.

There is one way to deal with any of these bits of waves and weather: recognize it for what it is, talk about it with someone, pray for peace and protection, then get on with it! Stay on target.

Waves and weather are part of any ministry that matters to God. They are part of all rich, real lives. If we commit our lives to God to be used, we will set off on adventures unimaginable. We'll run into challenges, growing pains, conflict, and distractions. But God called us into it and will not desert us. Other great sailors are in the ship with us. We aren't alone. We will endure wild rides, but if life with God weren't hard, it wouldn't be great!

The Holy and the Practical

Life with Christ is reality. It is joy. It is hope. It is salvation. It matters more than anything in the world. It is life that infuses and subsumes the world. In despair, we have hope in God. In fear, the shattering surrender of Christ on the cross shines live glory on us. This is the heart of faith. This is the good news.

Some moments of faith sink so deep they can't be described. They happen in the recesses of your soul. You may have felt some of them—being prayed for before surgery; sitting in candle-lit quiet in the Christmas Eve service; hearing the one phrase that unlocks your heart in a sermon written for you. Words cannot express the feelings of forgiveness, overwhelming love, resting in God in silent prayer. This is mystery and depth and holiness. This is what God has made known to us, and this is what Christ has asked us to show others.

Think. A soul is linked to a body. Evangelism is the same way. Sharing the mystery of God is a sacred gift contained in the practical structures of sermons and small groups, newcomer's dinner parties and signs for the parking lots. The holy is encased in the pragmatic.

Some churches are disconnected from the power and mystery of the holy. They live with details of Yellow Pages™ ads, but have nothing to share but muted friendliness and pale assurance. Other

---

Safety lies in God, not in our habits.

Evangelism Is Holiness Borne in Details

A soul is linked to a body. Evangelism is the same way. Sharing the mystery of God is a sacred gift contained in the practical structures of sermons and small groups, newcomer's dinner parties and signs for the parking lots. The holy is encased in the pragmatic.

churches, as the old African-American saying goes, are "so heavenly minded they're no earthly good." If you lose the mystery, you have nothing to share. If you don't focus and organize the sharing, the church turns inward.

So should we strike some nice average? A little mystery with a little detail and organization? Add the two extremes together, divide by two and live in the middle? I want to hear you shouting the words of Paul, "God forbid!" We'll end up lukewarm centrists like the church in Laodicea, and Jesus will want to throw up (Rev. 3:14–16). No! We have plenty of *those* churches already. Let's do something real instead.

Faith has to be real. Faith has to go as deeply into the holy mystery of life with God as we can stand. We are invited into give-it-all-away, bet-the-farm, choreographed-by-the-Spirit, life-walking-by-Christ's-side in minute-by-minute miraculous glory.

AND we've been given gifts of minds and hearts and computers and bread pans and nine irons and magic markers and QuickBooks® and singing voices and digital cameras. We've been given enthusiasm, relationships, minds, compassion, money and abilities to organize. All these joys and gifts and graces can live in and be utilized in a choreographed-by-the-Spirit life. *We have to hold the opposites together. It's All Mystery. It's All Practicality. All the time.*

Evangelism is holiness borne in details.

A Few Final Bits of Advice

A wonderful old Billy Graham pamphlet suggests thinking of the Bible as a love letter that God has sent to you, specifically to *you*. Don't let the Bible become a confusing, chaotic bundle of weird history, strange names and bizarre rules. Treasure it as a love letter God has written to you. Let's do something similar with our lives. See the faces of the people around you—at work, at the shoe store, at your son's Boy Scout meeting. Think:

"These are people Christ wants me to care for."

"I am God's love letter to them."

"And they are God's love letters to me."

What if your mailman; your mother-in-law; your neighbor with the incessantly barking sheltie; and every mink-clad, non-blinking, disastrously face-lifted shopper at the fancy mall were *exactly* the person Christ wants you to pray for right now? And maybe that person is the one God wants to use to teach you what *you* need to learn next.

Some churches are disconnected from the power and mystery of the holy. They live with details of Yellow Pages ads, but have nothing to share but muted friendliness and pale assurance. Other churches, in the old African-American saying, are "so heavenly-minded they're no earthly good." If you lose the mystery, you have nothing to share. If you don't focus and organize the sharing, the church turns inward.

If we live deeply with God, we will start to see fragmentary glimpses of people through Christ's eyes. A pastor told me, "The more I pray, the more I just *love* people with tattoos!" Once we have these glimmers of how God must see us, we want to help God care for those people; we want to learn from them.

Could life be different for the frazzled mother dragging her shrieking two-year-old away from the Twinkies™ display? Could God use you to bring a life-changing experience to the married businessman hitting on the flight attendant? To the lonely, brilliant physics student? How about the frazzled chef who snorts cocaine? What might be different for each of these people if they were living with Christ with the support of a church? Envision the difference Jesus could make in these people's lives. This "envisioning" is prayer. The prayer may open opportunities for you to listen or speak a word. The love, the prayer and the word are pure evangelism.

How can you support sustainable faith sharing in your life? In your church? Here are a few, practical ways:

1. The bedrock of sustainable Christian action is a spiritual life. Prayer, accountability, the study of scripture, history and theology matter. Commit yourself to a small group of Christians who study and pray together. Your individual prayer life is also crucial. You can start ministry without a prayer life, but soon it will be some combination of shallow, misdirected and burned out! *Please* don't try to skip this step.

2. Do what you love. Have you ever been arm-twisted into teaching the junior high Sunday school class out of duty? That hardly *ever* works out well. Don't get dragged into some slotted, pigeonholed job "doing evangelism." Reread the first story in chapter 2, about the group of women who formed an evangelism team at Benton Street Church. This story combines steps 1 and 2 here. First, pray. Second, don't do it if it's not fun! Do what you love. If you like baking bread, for heaven's sake don't head up the evangelism team. Bake bread! If you are a computer geek, volunteer to write software and keep systems going. Researchers should research things. People who love to teach should teach. Intercessors should intercede! Natural leaders should head up teams. Get the picture? Does a scripture occur to you here? (Hint: Ephesians 4 might be good!)

3. Learn to talk about your faith. All of us in churches have some sort of faith life. Will you join a class (or start a class) for people to learn and practice talking about their faith? Remember, evangelism isn't handing some pamphlet to a stranger. It's seeing who needs to

---

Faith has to be real. Faith has to go as deeply into the holy mystery of life with God as we can stand. We are invited into give-it-all-away, bet-the-farm, choreographed-by-the-Spirit, life-walking-by-Christ's-side in minute-by-minute miraculous glory.

be prayed for. It's waiting for an opening in a conversation with that friend to mention church or your faith. It can be as simple as, "You know, going to my church really helps me. Do you want to come to church with me on Sunday?" It can be more self-revealing, such as, "I know you feel guilty. I wish I didn't know so much about **that!** When I was…" Like anything else, practice makes it easier to do the next time.

4. Members of congregations do much more direct evangelism than pastors. Pastors preach and work with church members. They don't spend the day at IBM, the hardware store, the gym, the grade school or the golf course. People see *you*, not your pastor, as the person with the "real" faith life. You have credibility. You are the one with friends in the neighborhood. You are the one with a job in town, friends in classes. And no one sees you as the hired gun, paid to talk about God. Think of people in your life who have no one to pray for them. People you know, people you run into every day need different types of help. Many have no church to turn to. Could you start by praying for them? Then see what ideas the Spirit gives you.

5. Evangelists are all kinds of people. At the beginning of the Mainline Evangelism Project, I assumed that most of the people who helped non-Christians move into a faith life were like Bob Hope. No, not "Bing and Bob" Bob Hope, but a smiling, retired mechanic who was the heart of the Indianapolis-area church I served as pastor. Bob was one of the most loving, outgoing men I have ever known. Bob knew the name of every visitor who had ever set foot in the church. He had invited a third of them.

Bob drafted a bucket brigade out of the choir one Sunday morning between services. They filled the baptistry to hip height with tepid water from the kitchen sink and water heated on the stove. A junior high school student had the flu when she should have been baptized the week before. She had shown up for Sunday school and wanted to be baptized! I don't remember if the choir practiced the anthem. I do remember that we baptized Heather!

One afternoon, the church secretary walked into my office, laughing. She told me she had just seen Bob Hope at the grocery store loading 17 paper bags bulging with Pampers™, formula, and hotdog buns into the trunk of a young woman's car. The woman grinned feebly at Bob as she juggled a fractious four-year-old and a crying baby. The whole family appeared in church the next Sunday. Bob was a magnet for Christ and for our church. I don't know whom he's evangelizing in heaven, but I want to hear *those* stories!

When our lives with God are stagnant, we are much more likely to impose rules, smother with sentimentality, or spout arid concepts. A vivid faith has power and moves. It carries the freight of the Gospel.

I have thought of Bob Hope as the "real" kind of evangelist ever since. Then along came the Mainline Evangelism Project, which gave me a surprise. I asked hundreds of people to describe the great evangelists in their congregation. People usually mentioned the pastor, then a person like Bob Hope first. But then I often heard, "Well, this is sort of strange, but there's this very shy woman [...quiet man,...little kid,...awkward high school student,...science librarian who barely talks above a whisper]..."

The stories are amazing. Often the pastor or evangelism team leaders didn't know that these shy ladies, gawky kids, nonverbal librarians had **anything** to do with the visitors arriving on the doorstep. Sometimes the people "in charge" heard the stories years later. Occasionally, churches asked new members for feedback and found out that way.

When finally asked what they were doing, these quiet people described praying for friends, neighbors and coworkers. God often showed the shy evangelists situations of a kid getting beaten up in school, a coworker going through a divorce, a neighbor's daughter needing a pastor to perform her wedding. The quiet evangelists placed phone calls and wrote little notes. They invited these people to church. And the beaten-up kid; the divorced husband; and the neighbor, her daughter and new son-in-law become Christians and begin their own adventures with Christ.

Typical pattern for the human part of evangelism:

- pastors hold up vision of evangelism, oversee implementation
- church members learn to talk about faith, find ways to share it
- bishops make evangelism a priority, encourage experimentation

6. New Christians as evangelists. We learned that new Christians' first desire is to learn the faith. They fall in love with God. They absorb the way Christianity makes the world make sense. They try to become more Christlike. They tell their friends—Microsoft executives, rock band guitarists, nursing home residents, Chinese historians, tenth graders and soccer coaches. Mainly, they're learning. Evangelistic churches nurture this growth and understand how tender it is.

Typical churches say that new members do most of their evangelism. I am sure that is true. But that may say more about typical churches' lack of focus on evangelism than about who does the most inviting and faith sharing in a healthy church! Our study demonstrated that in the high adult baptism churches, it's the longer-term members who are doing most of the inviting and faith sharing.

Our newest members, our newest Christians, should be able to share their faith. They are usually very enthusiastic about their new faith/new church. Many of their friends are not Christians. They can help us see what we can do to be more welcoming to their friends. But we must let them grow up. We must not burden them with responsibilities until they are ready. Their enthusiasm will encourage everyone. Just go gently. Don't create a "New Members as Prey" scenario! New Christians' first priority is learning the faith and connecting with the church.

7. We long-time members aren't prey, either! Devote at least a quarter of each church group or meeting to prayer and sharing about your own lives. Every financial committee, board meeting, class, work group or mission trip should be your small group, your prayer group. If we talk about our own lives, study scripture and pray together, God can work through us more directly. If we're open to God and in spiritual agreement, we don't block out the Spirit as much. Try this in every church meeting for three months and you'll see— praying is not a waste of time.

Really.

8. Pray for the people who have no one to pray for them. Dwight Ozard, a young, brilliant, evangelical music lover; dark chocolate fanatic; author; church consultant and wild, free spirit was a friend. He died too soon after a long struggle with cancer. He ended every e-mail, "Thanks for praying for Sheri and me, but please also pray for all the unnamed people with no one to pray for them."

Remember, Christian sisters and brothers: You are the only person whose life touches all of the people you know, work with and meet every day. You may be the only one praying for them. You may be the person Christ has put in their lives to help. We can pray for the ones we don't know yet whom God could use us to help. Evangelism is about relationships. All relationships are in God's hands. So are all people. Prayer and awareness can lead us into amazing places.

Your only job is to let Jesus love you, do the best you can pretty much of the time, and be willing to listen to the Spirit so that you can be used by Christ. God can work unimaginable miracles with that!

Jesus Is the Answer; So <u>What</u> Is the Question?

You've finished this chapter. And if you have been praying with the meditations that follow along with each chapter, you are also finishing the book. Now you're ready for a new beginning. I'm trying to think of a final word, a final paragraph that might help launch each of us into this next year of our lives with God. Do you remember the questions with which we started this book? Why *do* evangelism? What's motivating *you*? What difference does being a Christian make in *your* life? How could it matter in someone else's life? Do you have clearer answers to those questions than when you started reading this book? I hope so.

A bumper sticker in the '70s and '80s proclaimed, "Jesus Is the Answer." I have a vivid memory of getting a ride home from law school with a couple of friends. We had just escaped from five hours of grilling by law school professors. The day had been a mix of boredom punctuated with random moments of terror. Professors had an uncharitable tendency to fire sudden salvos at the jokers in the back row. "Ms. Reese, what is the critical point upon which Justice Brandeis' argument for the dissent turns?" I usually maneuvered for time to think by rising slowly to my feet, saying, "Excuse me, sir, would you mind rephrasing the question?" Eventually, I had to stand in front of 90 classmates and try to bumble out a coherent answer, at the expense of my entire nervous system.

It had been a long day. Now we were cruising home. A traffic light turned yellow. The rattletrap car in front of us gunned the accelerator, then screeched to a stop. My friend slammed on the brakes, swearing. The bumper sticker gleamed from the stopped car's rear bumper: "*Jesus Is the Answer*." My friend muttered under his breath, "So *what* was the question?"

I realized at the time, after a day of being pummeled by questions, that my friend was right. It *matters* which question is asked. I realize more clearly today, decades later, that knowing the question to which Jesus is the answer unlocks the universe. What's the question Jesus answers? What's the problem a life with Jesus solves? We need to know. The church has asked this question for nearly 2000 years. We say, "Jesus saves us." The question is, "*From what* does Jesus save us?"

What is the biggest problem of human existence? From what does Jesus save us? Sin? Yes. Jesus saves us from sin. Some parts of the church focus strongly on sin as the main problem. Other churches see death as the biggest human problem. Jesus saves us from death, too. Some parts of the church look at the biggest human problem as distorted human community that draws us away from God and truth. They know that Jesus can heal community, miraculously transform isolated individuals and sick societies.

Sin, death, demonic social conditions—they're all pivotal human questions. They are questions rooted deeply in scripture. Clearly, Jesus can save us from each of them. Jesus is the answer to all of these human problems. We know this from scripture, from theology, from human experience. Jesus saves us from sin. Salvation is forgiveness, healing and union with God. Jesus saves us from death. Salvation is life forever with God. Jesus saves and heals human communities: families, churches, neighborhoods, countries. Whatever our individual or communal presenting problems—sin, confusion, illness, loneliness,

Envision the difference Jesus could make in these people's lives. This "envisioning" is prayer. The prayer may open opportunities for you to listen or speak a word. The love, the prayer and the word are pure evangelism.

isolation, poverty, violence, drugs, death—God can save us through Christ. No space in the human psyche is too small for God's healing through Christ. No far point of the universe is beyond the Spirit's whisper of forgiveness, the creative life of God's touch.

The deeper our lives, the more we dwell in scripture, the more alive our prayer, the more thoughtful our reflections, the more conscious our relationship with God, the richer our community experience, the more clearly we will see the questions. And the more we can see that Jesus is the answer. We can live shallow lives. God is there, luring us deeper. When we move into more complex realms of life, God is there, giving us comfort and glimpses of mystery; enticing us further in, higher up. More layers await us. A life of faith has no glass ceiling. The waters that flow into the well of life with God are infinite.

We can never outgrow God or outgrow faith. We can test the limits, ask the questions of Job, challenge each other, wrestle with God. What is the deepest place in your soul? Open your inner eye—you will see Christ there. We can never reach beyond the limits of God or of God's love for us. What question wracks your being? Jesus is the answer. What questions are other people asking? Are they lonely? Are they guilty? Are they afraid? Are they angry? Jesus is the answer. The path to loving community, to forgiveness, to peace, to rest, to healing, to resolution, to justice lies in a growing relationship with God. Jesus is the answer. This is the Good News.

Are you going to tell someone?

Pastors' Advice for Bishops:

- Make evangelism a real priority!
- Encourage experimentation

DISCUSSION QUESTIONS _____

1. Begin your time together by praying for each other. How has everyone's private prayer gone this week?

2. Is there a Bible passage that came to mind when you read this chapter, or that occurs to you now? Discuss how it connects with what you have read. (If no passages come to mind, you might want to look at: Philippians 4:6–7; Isaiah 30:19–21; 1 Corinthians 9:24–27; Mark 4:35–41; Matthew 28:18–20.)

3. Discuss how you have changed during these last six weeks. How has your prayer life changed? How has your thinking about the "E-word" changed? How have your feelings about evangelism changed? Have your habits shifted? What have you done differently? What will you do differently in the next week or so?

At the beginning of each session:

A. Light a candle to remind us of Christ's presence;

B. Repeat aloud, together: **"We agree that we will hold everything shared in this group in complete confidence."**

4. Which insights from chapter 6 are most applicable to your church? Discuss this. Then write down your group's ideas for practical steps your congregation could take to share your faith more effectively. Give them to your pastor or study coordinator. Your church's leadership will compile all the groups' ideas for everyone to see. Then the leadership will think and pray about the ideas and come up with some navigational charts.

Now: Cast off! Start sailing!

EXERCISE

Sit quietly with each other and with God for a few minutes. In your mind, ask the Spirit for an idea, an inspiration of what you can do, either as a person or together, to share your faith. Draw a picture or write down the images or words you receive. Talk together about each person's inspiration. Ask someone to keep a record of what the Spirit shows each person.

What has your group learned from this six weeks? Let each one name the thing for which you are most grateful. Pray for each other. Pray for your church. Pray for the people God is preparing to receive a Word through you. Amen.

---

[1] *The Godfather,* directed by Francis Ford Coppola, Paramount, 1972.

[2] Kenneth C. Haugk, *Antagonists in the Church: How to Identify and Deal with Destructive Conflict* (Minneapolis: Augsburg, 1988), 25–26.

[3] *Star Wars: Episode IV–A New Hope,* 20th Century Fox, 1977.

PART THREE

■ **PART ONE** focuses on *what is* and on *what can be* for individuals and for churches.

■ **PART TWO** helps you see your church more clearly and start to move toward new possibilities.

■ **PART THREE** is your 40-day, individual prayer journal. Use it on your own each day. You can discuss it each week when you meet with your study group.

Look, I have set before you an open door, which no one is able to shut. (Rev. 3:8a)

Your 40-Day Prayer Journal

Welcome to your own time with God, a page for each day for six weeks. Let's start with a confession—mine. I talk *such* a good game about prayer, but doing it isn't always so easy. I swoop eagle-like on currents of glorious inspiration—every once in a while. But many days I'd rather talk than pray, read than pray, change the oil in the car than pray. I possess impressive avoidance mechanisms to shield myself from going face-to-Face with God. And yet, I *have* developed a daily prayer discipline.

I've learned not to wait to brush my teeth until I am moved by a spontaneous burst of creativity. I don't wait to exercise until I am smitten with a wild desire to lift the dreaded weights. It's pretty much the same with prayer. I've learned that my life is better if I pray every day. Other people's lives are better if I pray every day. So at 5:30 almost every morning, we're up praying at our house. On the other days, I pray when I take long walks or paddle my kayak. So if you have tendencies to think, "I'll pray in an hour...I'll pray after I organize my sock drawer...I'll pray tomorrow—at Tara," here are daily prayer exercises from a kindred spirit. They may help you get into the habit of praying. I promise—it's worth the effort.

Why Pray?

Good prayer habits act like an incubator for our relationships with God. If we pray, if we show up, God has a much better chance of getting through to us. Over time, we know ourselves and know God better. I have great news: prayer affects more than you! Our research demonstrates that when people pray, talk with a prayer partner, and talk about faith with others at church, something exciting happens. Relationships improve. Families tend to get happier. People who pray mysteriously "have the words" when the Holy Spirit arranges situations for them to talk with people who don't have a conscious faith life. Prayer helps us *listen* to other people for real.

Prayer changes things—within us and for others.

We're probably not going to slip one day and fall into Christian maturity. Prayer is about developing a relationship with God, not just "believing in God." God is consistent with us! Could we learn to be consistent with God? Are you ready to get started? Leaf through this section of *Unbinding Your Heart* and see if it looks inviting to you. Take a moment in the quiet (or several days) to ask yourself if the Spirit is nudging you to commit to this prayer habit.

Are you ready to try—for yourself, and for what God can do for others through *you*?

Will you try to pray consistently for six weeks? If you agree to try, sign here:

Signature:_____Date:_____

Prayer Partner

Talking about your reaction to these exercises with someone else from your small group at church, a neighborhood friend, someone in your retirement community or your family will maximize the benefit of your six weeks of prayer. A mother told me, "We are praying together in the morning and talking about what God's showing us at dinner [two parents, a very active second grader and two junior high school kids]. We all love the prayers, scriptures and exercises for different reasons. Doing this together is awesome—it's helping us understand each other better and love each other even more." Whatever your living situation, please talk about your response to these exercises with at least one other person, once a week, in person or by phone. Budget at least a "check-in" time about your prayer when your *Unbinding Your Heart* study group meets each week. Half the fun is getting to see how everyone's individual prayer is progressing.

Prayers for Can't-Sit-Still *and* Artistic Types!

Not everyone thinks, works, learns or prays the same way. Some people are highly creative and learn best when they use their hands, voices, bodies. Do what you works for you—do what you love. Draw, act out parts, sculpt a model of the scripture! Some of us pray best while moving or talking. My ADHD (attention deficit hyperactivity disorder) friends have fits when they even *think* about sitting in one place in silence. ***Our motto is: give new ways to pray a chance, but pray in the ways that work for you!*** This prayer journal offers you 40 days of varied prayer exercise suggestions. I could never list all the options, but here are a few:

- Walk around the room while you read the scripture, timing the words with your steps or your breath
- Read the scripture out loud or write it out
- "Act out" the Bible story
- DRAW or form a Play-doh™ figure of the scripture
- Read the scripture sitting, then pray walking. Return to your chair to sketch or write notes.

I include a "Notes, Lists, Drawings, Thoughts, Insights" section for each day. Write a list, sketch a drawing, do whatever makes the day's exercise most effective and memorable to you. Experiment. Have fun with it. If you don't know what you want to do, ask God. You may be surprised at some of the nudges you get from the Spirit!

Same Time, Same Place

Choose a specific time to try to pray each day. Although I have written as if you are praying early in the morning, you may be drawn to a time after breakfast, when everyone else has left the house; lunch time in your office; or evening (instead of TV or before bed). If in doubt, ask God what time you should choose. Don't drive yourself crazy about exact adherence to A Rigid Plan, but consistency will help you develop the habit of prayer! Light a candle each day as you sit down if you wish, to remind yourself that Christ is right there with you. You can develop simple habits that will help you grow in your relationship with God.

William Law, a wise eighteenth-century English theologian and writer, influenced generations of pastors, including the Wesleys, from whose work the Methodist churches began. Law suggested that we have one special chair in which to pray each day. Choose a (not too) comfortable, straight-backed chair in a room away from family traffic patterns. Only pray and do your devotions in this chair during these six weeks—no mystery novels, no TV, no phones, no iPods,™ no directing kids' homework! Keep your supplies right next to your chair so you don't have to interrupt your prayer time to go get something.

Supplies

I would keep these supplies right by your prayer chair:

- Bible
- Pens, pencils, art supplies, clay
- Reading glasses
- This book
- Prayer candle and matches
- Journal or extra writing paper
- 3 x 5" cards

A few days contain suggestions for using a few supplies. Plan ahead for:

- ▲ *Week 2, Day 4:* Address book or PDA & your city phone book
- ▲ *Week 4, Day 5:* a string of pearls, beads, Mardi Gras beads, or prayer beads

Bible Readings

Each prayer day starts with a scripture. Scripture means "writing." In this case I'm referring to a passage from the Christian Bible. The Bible contains two main parts, the "Old Testament," sometimes called the "Hebrew Scriptures." They were originally written in the Hebrew language. These scriptures were all written before Jesus was born. We date our years as starting with Jesus' birth at time point zero and his death in year 33. The second part of the Christian Bible is called the "New Testament" or the "Greek Scriptures." This part was written (in Greek) about Jesus' life, death and resurrection. The New Testament was written *after* Jesus' death and resurrection, between the years 55 and 125 A.D. (After [Jesus'] Death), or C.E. (Common Era).

You may have studied the Bible for years and feel very comfortable with biblical literature and history. You may not own a Bible. If you don't have a Bible, could you ask your pastor or the person leading your group where to get one and which translation they'd suggest? I would suggest a study Bible, because they explain things.

I list a scripture for each day by the name of the "book" of the Bible (often the name of the person who wrote it). The first number after the name of the book is the number of the chapter. Then there's a colon (:). The next number is the number of the verse in the chapter. Most Bibles include a list of the books of the Bible somewhere near the front. The books consist of different types of writings—histories, letters of advice, poetry, writings from prophets and "Gospels," which are stories about Jesus' life. Your Bible may have tabs on the side so you can get to different books quickly.

Don't be a hero! Don't gut this out alone. ***Loads*** of people have questions about the Bible, and lots of them have been sitting in church for 20 years. Ask for help ***before*** you get frustrated or feel awkward! If you aren't sure how to locate the scripture readings, ask your group leader or best friend in the class to mark the next week's passages in your Bible with Post-it[R] notes—no fuss, no muss and no lost time! (Read the notes in your study Bible—they're fascinating.) You'll learn a bit about the Bible, and get right on to the fun part—actually ***reading*** the scriptures and praying!

As You Pray Each Day

Sit in your chair. Light a candle if you wish. Breathe deeply and slowly. Close your eyes and ask Christ (or God, or the Spirit) to help you pray. Ask God to help you understand whatever you need to see next. Then, when you feel centered, read the entire day's exercise to familiarize yourself with it. Finally, take a deep breath, exhale, read the scripture and begin!

Keep the Main Thing the Main Thing!

The point of these prayer exercises is to help you pray with scripture, move closer to God and grow as a Christian. If you are drawn into a certain phrase of scripture, if you feel a sense of God's presence one day or get "caught" by one idea—stick with it! Our increasing awareness of the presence of God is what matters in our spiritual lives. The exercises are only a tool to help you try new ways of being more receptive to the Spirit. If you and God are drawn into a "side conversation," it's probably the main thing. Stay with God, not the program!

Christ loves us. He loves it when we try to mature in our relationship with him. Our prayers help us. Our prayers help others more than we will know. Ready to move into this faith adventure? All right, let's go!

How Do You Know God?

Scripture: Psalm 139:1–12

Light your candle if you'd like. Take some slow, deep breaths and relax. Sit quietly for a few moments and ask God to bless this six-week prayer adventure.

God is huge, unfathomable. Christ knows and loves us so intimately. ***Unbinding Your Heart*** is about faith sharing. But our faith is in a God who is vast, mysterious and very different than we are. How can we talk about our fumbling understandings of such a God? The more our faith means to us, the less we want to reduce it to bumper-sticker portability!

We can learn to begin to talk about our faith authentically because God has shown us Godself through scripture and through the life, the death and the resurrection of Jesus. We can learn to talk about our faith because God will speak to us moment-by-moment through the Spirit. The Spirit will give us words.

Will you read the Psalm slowly? Which lines speak to you most powerfully? Sit quietly for a moment. Now read the Psalm again, slowly. What words or phrases shine out at you? Mark them in your Bible or jot them down here.

How do you know God? Close your eyes a moment and ask God to show you again the moments, the ways in your life when you have seen or understood or experienced God most clearly. What are your deepest moments of faith? A conversion experience? A tiny moment of awe during a Christmas Eve service? A nudge from the Spirit? A powerful insight during a sermon or reading the Bible? A healing? A knowledge of forgiveness? Everyone's experiences of God are different. Ask God to show you yours. Write down what feels most important.

Notes, lists, drawings, ideas:

Prayer: God, you are the Holy One of Israel, Creator of the Universe, so majestic we cannot possibly understand you. And Jesus told us to call you "Daddy" because you love us so much. Thank you for my life and for my family and friends and the people you can use me to help. Please let me know you better as I go through these next six weeks. I offer you this time. Amen.

Build an Altar

Scripture: Genesis 12:1–9

This is the beginning of the story of Sarah and Abraham, the father and mother of all the Jews and, because of our faith, our spiritual great-great-great...grandfather and mother. They are 66 and 75 years old. God calls them to leave home behind, to set out on a trip, in some ways similar to this next 39 days for us. God promises that he will bless them and give them a land and children. They packed up and left the life they had known. In verse 7 and in verse 8, Abram builds altars to God. Abraham and Sarah symbolically offer God everything—their obedience, their lives, their decisions.

You've answered God's call to start out on a faith journey, too. Will you stop now and imagine building an altar to God? Read this, then close your eyes and imagine. God has called you here, into this chair, into this room, into this quiet. See yourself slowly building an altar. Find rocks. Pick them up. Carry them to the right place. Carefully stack them.

Then ask God if there is anything you can put on the altar. Is there anything you could hand over that would please God? An opinion? A sin? A habit? Something you want? Your time? Ask the Spirit if there is anything you are using to keep God at a safe distance.

Place your gifts on the altar. Light the match. Light the gifts, and watch them burn, crackle and spark into the night sky.

Notes, lists, drawings, ideas:

Prayer: Oh, Lord. Here is what I think you'd like me to offer you on my altar. Please accept these gifts, these sacrifices. Please show me if there's anything else I can give you that would help me see you more clearly. In these forty days, please let me know myself better and know you better. Please let me begin to understand how much you love me. Amen.

A Thank You Note to God

Scripture: 1 Thessalonians 1–5; Philippians 4:4–7

St. Paul opens letters with thanksgiving and rejoicing. Paul closes letters with thanksgiving and rejoicing. He rejoices in what God has done. He rejoices in salvation. He gives thanks for the work of the Spirit. He gives thanks for the church people and the ministry they are doing for Christ. Paul teaches, he encourages, he diagnoses, he blasts, he charms, he rants, he sings powerfully and poetically about what a Christian life can be. But Paul always thanks people. He always thanks God.

We live way too quickly. We race to meetings, blast horns, prioritize and multitask. Very few of us write thank you notes. Few of us slow down enough to see the blessings of our lives, or God's presence in our lives.

Do you remember how much fun it was when you were a kid and drew a grid on your hand to play tic-tac-toe in class? Remember drawing a face on your fisted hand, where the mouth was the space between your thumb and first knuckle? Try something fun as you go through your day today. Make a little ink mark on your hand today every time you see God's presence, a kindness, a blessing. (Okay, okay, if you're a bank president or work in a suit, you can put the marks under your sleeve or on a 3 x 5 card in your pocket!)

At the end of the day, look at your hand. Remember. Write something about it here. Would it be good to write a thank you note to a person? Do it. Would it be good to write a thank you note to God? Please do.

Notes, lists, drawings, ideas:

Prayer:

God be in my head and my understanding,
God be in my eyes and in my looking,
God be in my mouth and in my speaking;
God be in my heart and in my thinking;
God be at my end and in my departing.

from the Sarum Missal, 11th century, Salisbury, England

Prayer for the Children

Scripture: Mark 10:13–16

Jesus loved children. The gospels (the New Testament books that tell the story of the life of Jesus) tell many stories about Jesus with children, healing children, bringing a little girl back to life, and Jesus himself as a child. We see Jesus first as a baby in a manger. Children are precious to God.

One of the great gifts of praying is to pray for others. This is called "intercessory prayer." Let's start with the children. Picture a child. Imagine you're holding him/her between your hands, or on your lap. Ask Christ to surround that child with love, protection and healing. Pray for the child's safety, for growing maturity. Pray that the child will come to know Jesus, now and every step of the way as s/he grows. Pray that Christ's love and protection will radiate out from the child to his family, to her school, to his friends and their families.

Two prayer options:

(A) Pray this way for the children you know. Pray for children in your church's pictorial directory. Pray for the children you don't know yet, but that you and your church could reach in the next year. Pray that God will prepare them, their families and your church to care for them. Pray for one child and ask God to use your prayer to bless *all* children.

(B) Take a field trip. Go walk around a school in your neighborhood. As you circle the sidewalk around the school, pray for the safety, health and spiritual growth of every child, teacher and staff person in the school. Pray that all the children come to know God in whatever way God wants to reach them. Feel that you are encircling the children, their families, the staff and the school with Christ's love, presence and protection with every step you take.

Notes, lists, drawings, ideas:

Prayer: God, please let every child know your love, health and safety. All of us in our church today pray for the children we know…for children with too many possessions and too little attention…for children of single parents…for children who are ill or in danger…for children on the other side of the world—in Africa, in Asia, in the Middle East. May all the children know health, safety, loving training and You. Amen.

What Difference Does It Make That I'm a Christian?

Scripture: Luke 9:18–27

Jesus has been many things to many people for nearly two millennia. This passage shows who some crowd members thought Jesus was—"Elijah," "a prophet risen from the dead," "John the Baptist." When Jesus asked the disciples what they thought, Peter answered with what we've come to call "the Great Confession." Peter said, "you are the Messiah of God." Then Jesus told the disciples that to be his followers, they would join in his suffering and rejection, take up their crosses daily and follow him.

Most of us are not very clear about who Jesus is. What do you think? Is Jesus a great teacher for you? A great prophet? A vague, historical figure of holiness or comfort? An example of kindness and service? Your savior? What does he save you from? Does he walk beside you?

Do you think of yourself as a Christian? What practical difference does that make in your life? What real difference does it make that you are a Christian?

Close your eyes and ask Christ to show you what being his disciple means in your life. Ask him to show you what you could learn next. Invite the Spirit to show you the next step you could take.

Notes, lists, drawings, ideas:

Prayer: Holy One—I'm only scratching the surface of what it means to be a Christian. Will you show me what I can do to be a better disciple, a real follower? Please show me the steps and give me the courage to walk them with you. Amen.

Reflection Day

REVIEW. Think back over your week of prayer. Reread your favorite scripture from the week. Review your notes, lists, insights. How is your prayer going? Review the introduction to Part Three, beginning on page 115. Which ideas from the introduction do you need to pay attention to this week? Take some notes.

Then, answer two questions:

Question 1: What are the most important things I've learned/discovered/remembered this week?

Question 2: God, what one insight would you like me to share with my study group when we meet?

Prayer:

Oh yes, fix me, Jesus, fix me.
Fix me so that I can walk on a little while longer.
Fix me so that I can pray on just a little bit harder.
Fix me so that I can sing on just a little bit louder.
Fix me so that I can go on despite the pain, the fear, the doubt and, yes, the anger.
I ask not that you take this cross from me,
only that you give me the strength to continue carrying it onward 'til my dying day.
Oh, fix me, Jesus, fix me.

"Fix Me, Jesus, Fix Me," African-American Spiritual

Group Meeting Day

Enjoy your time together! Tell each other what you've learned. Talk about your *Unbinding the Gospel chapter.* Pray together.

Notes & insights from your group time:

Prayer: Holy God, thank you for this beautiful day of rest.
Glory be to the Father and to the Son and to the Holy Ghost. As it was in the beginning, is now and ever shall be, world without end. Amen.

Ancient Prayer, Gloria Patri

God's Love in Christ

Scripture: Romans 8:35–39

Will you read these words as a love letter from God?

Sit quietly for a minute, breathing slowly, letting go of thoughts and feelings. Just be with God for a minute. As you inhale, then exhale, feel as if you are living in the very center of your body, where you breathe.

Now read St. Paul's words slowly. Which lines speak to you most powerfully?

Sit in the silence with God for several more minutes. Now read the scripture again, slowly. What words strike you as most important? Gleam out at you? Offer God several more minutes of silence. Just be with God. What do you notice?

Notes, drawings, thoughts:

Prayer: Lord Jesus, thank you. Thank you that nothing can separate me from you. Amen.

Reaching to Jesus

Scripture: Mark 5:24b–34

Sit quietly, breathe deeply. Exhale slowly. Then slowly read this story about Jesus and the woman with the hemorrhage. Pay close attention to the details.

We all have places in our lives that are bleeding. What is yours? Are you lonely? Tired? Discouraged? Physically ill? Angry? Bitter? Jealous? Have you judged someone for something they did to you? Your judgment can anchor their sin into your soul with a spiritual fishhook.

Sit quietly, then read the story again. Ask God what in you needs to be healed. Offer it to God. When you are ready, reach forward to touch Jesus.

Notes, drawings, thoughts:

Prayer: Lord Jesus, I offer you my_____

_____, this

unhealed part of me. Thank you. Thank you for healing. Amen.

A Prayer Walk

Scripture: Genesis 1:26—2:3

God loves creation. God made us, the animals, our beautiful earth. There are actually two stories of creation in the book of Genesis. This is the end of the first one (from Gen. 1 and 2), which tells of God creating the world in seven days. At the end of each day, God looked at everything he made that day and said it was good. The other creation story is the Adam and Eve story (Gen. 2 and 3). In that story, God walked around the garden of Eden "at the time of the evening breeze" (Gen. 3:8). Both of these powerful stories show God's joy in what God has brought into being. God is still creating.

We can join God in that joy and care-taking. Today, take a "Prayer Walk." Choose a place—whether in nature, a shopping mall, your office, the library, the grimy bus station downtown, your own neighborhood or someone else's. Walk through it slowly. Try to see it with God's eyes. Feel God's love for the place, the growing things, the people. As you walk, bless the houses, or rooms or paths. Bless the people who will go in and out of them, their families. Pray for God's healing, guidance, protection. Pray as you feel the Spirit moving you to pray for anyone you see. What did you notice?

Notes, drawings, thoughts:

Prayer: O God, thank you for that glimpse of the way you see us and this amazing world. I pray again for each person I saw, for their families, for their needs. Protect each one. Please heal our sin and brokenness. Help each one to come to know you as fully as we humans can. In the name of Jesus Christ, I pray. Amen.

Plain Old Names

Supplies: Address Book or PDA, City Phone Book

Scripture: Matthew 1:1–17

Read the scripture. Wow! Isn't that stunningly boring? All those names are so ***tedious***. Then you realize those names are really people. Each one of them had whole lives, with everything that goes into a life: joy, suffering, fear, awe, gratitude, hoarded resentments, learning, laughter, pain, anger, forgiveness, love. Matthew sums up 42 generations of people—their lives, their relationships with people, their relationships with God—using a list of 42 first names.

Now, put the phone book and your list of addresses in your lap. Close your eyes and begin to breathe quietly and deeply. Feel Jesus' power and protection surrounding you. Be in the stillness with Christ for as long as you want to.

When you are ready, turn your attention to the names in your lap. There are thousands of names, thousands of lives, thousands of families, represented there. Bring them into the stillness of God with you. Pray that they share God's peace. Let the Spirit guide your prayer for them.

Notes, drawings, thoughts:

Prayer: Lord Jesus, you came from the 42 generations that started with Abraham and Sarah and stretched on to Joseph and Mary. You came from Israel and you are now with me, sitting here, and with all these people whose names I hold up to you right now. Keep us. Save us. Help us all move into real life with you. Amen.

A Gift of Christ's Love

Scripture: 1 John 3:14–24

Sit quietly and ask the Spirit of Christ to be with you. Rest in Christ for a minute or two. When you feel ready to be open to the Word of God, read this beautiful portion of the first letter of John. Love is the watchword, the sign of the Christian. Being in Christ means that the love of Christ lives in us. When we know Christ's love, the Spirit will prompt us in words and acts of love. Reread this scripture and ponder the words in your heart.

Will you close your eyes and ask Christ if there is someone whom he would like you to give something to show his love today? A name or a face may appear to you as you pray. If no one occurs to you during your prayer, ask the Spirit to prompt you as you go through your day. Who is it? What is the gift? As you move through the day, be sensitive to the promptings of the Spirit. Does that homeless man need a sandwich from Subway™? Is your neighbor lonely? Should you endow a scholarship for a needy child? Does someone need a phone call, a card, a bit of encouragement, a job? Ask the Spirit. When the time is right, give the person Christ's gift.

Notes, drawings, thoughts:

Prayer: Beloved Christ, please let me know you and your love better. Please help me show your face to people who need to see you. Amen.

Reflection Day

REVIEW. Think back over your week of prayer. Reread your favorite scripture from the week. Review your notes, lists, insights. How is your prayer going? Review the introduction to Part Three, beginning on page 115. Which ideas from the introduction do you need to pay attention to this week? Take some notes.

Then, answer two questions:

Question 1: What are the most important things I've learned/discovered/remembered this week?

Question 2: God, what one insight would you like me to share with my study group when we meet?

Prayer: Lord, remember not only the [people] of good will, but also those of ill will. But do not remember all the suffering they have inflicted upon us. Remember rather the fruits we have brought thanks to this suffering: our comradeship, our loyalty, our humility, the courage, the generosity, the greatness of heart that has grown out of this. And when they come to judgment, let all the fruits we have borne be their forgiveness.

Found on a scrap of paper at the liberation of Ravensbruck Concentration Camp
20th Century, Germany

Group Meeting Day

Enjoy your time to talk, laugh and pray together! Tell each other what you've learned. Pray together.

Notes, thoughts & insights:

Prayer:

Praise God from whom all blessings flow.

Praise God, all creatures here below.

Praise God above, ye heavenly hosts.

Praise Father, Son and Holy Ghost. Amen.

1674 version of the Doxology, an ancient prayer from the Greek and Latin churches, by Thomas Ken

An Hour for the Spirit

Scripture: John 14:16–26

When you think of God, do you think first of the HUGE God who created the universe, the God on the ceiling of the Sistine Chapel, the God "Out There?" I think many people think first of the God of majesty and mystery, of awe and power, the "transcendent" God. But we also talk about the "immanent" God who's right here with us, in the middle of groups of us, inside each one of us. That's "God *with* us." Jesus in the manger, Jesus who walked on earth, Jesus who is risen and walks beside us, and also the Holy Spirit

Read John 14:16–26. Jesus was preparing his disciples for his death and resurrection. He told them he would be with them in a different way after his death. God would send the Spirit. The Holy Spirit is available to *us,* because *we're* Jesus' disciples too. Jesus offers us guidance, power, minute-by-minute connection with God. This isn't some nice little metaphor. Life in the Spirit is more like plugging into an electric current!

Powerful Christians, mystics, prophets and missionaries have sensed the power and subtle leading of the Holy Spirit for thousands of years now. Too many of us leave God at arm's length, "up in the sky," a vaguely comforting idea, but not too real. Would you be willing to try an experiment? The intent of this isn't to minimize the majesty of God, but to help us see that we can turn to God every moment of the day. The Spirit is with us.

Experiment: Choose an hour of your day today when you're going to offer every choice to God. Each minute of this hour, ask God what you're supposed to be seeing, what you're supposed to do next. It could be an hour at the office—should you talk with someone? Make a phone call? Sort those papers? Bless the lunch room? Ask the Spirit to guide your decisions. If it's the first hour of the day, which side of the bed should you get out of? Should you wash your face or brush your teeth first? Ask which child you should kiss first. Before you open your mouth to speak, ask the Spirit to give you the words to say. Oatmeal or Raisin Bran? This isn't about the cosmic importance of cereal. It's about the cosmic importance of what God can do with us if we learn to offer the daily stuff to God.

Ask. Then do it. What happened?

Notes, drawings, thoughts:

Prayer: God, of your goodness, give me yourself, for you are sufficient for me... If I were to ask anything less I should always be in want, for in you alone do I have all.

Julian of Norwich, 14th century, England

Remembering Your Day

Scripture: Psalm 51:6–12

Sit quietly for a few moments. Breathe deeply; exhale your troubles. Feel what is true: you are sitting in the very heart of God.

Now read the Psalm slowly. God will purify us, heal us, restore and sustain a willing spirit in us. Take the words of the Psalm into your own heart. Sit in silence for a moment, then ask God to re-walk through your last day with you. Ask God to help you remember each moment of grace, of blessing, of God's presence that occurred during the day. Write them down in a list. Thank God for each of them.

After you have seen these moments of divine presence and blessing, ask God to show you the moment during the day when you were farthest from God, the moment you would most like to do differently. Ask God's forgiveness. Give thanks and ask to go into this next day forgiven, restored and new.

Notes, drawings, thoughts:

Prayer: Oh Holy One, thank you for the graces and blessings you have given me today. Thank you for your forgiveness. Create in me a clean heart. Restore me to the joy of your salvation. Sustain in me a generous, willing spirit. Amen.

My Best Memory of Church

Scripture: Colossians 3:12–17

Yesterday you asked God to walk you through the day. Today is the day to think about your church. (If you haven't been there very long, you can think about another church. If you haven't been a Christian very long, you can think about your experiences with Christians. If there's another category I missed, go for it!)

Read this beautiful scripture about what church should be, can be. Sit in silence for a while and ask Christ to let you review in your mind the most beautiful memories you have ever had in church, the ones that matter the most. Sit silently for several minutes and look at the photo album that Christ will show you.

Now, pray for the church—pretend you are holding the whole church in your hands. Hold it gently and pray for it. Pray for the building, pray for the people, pray for the pastors. Pray for the congregation's past. Pray for right now. Pray for its future. Pray for yourself in the church. Pray for all the people who aren't there yet, but who might be if God and the church call them there.

Close by asking Christ's hands to surround the church and hold it safe now, and before and hereafter. Pray that your church will become the church in Colossians 3.

Notes, drawings, thoughts:

Prayer: Christ, thank you for the church. We fail, but we repent. Please saturate us with your Spirit. Let us be the most ***real*** church we can be. Let us become the church this scripture shows us. Amen.

Steps to Heaven, then Back to Earth

Scripture: Genesis 28:10–22

This is the beginning of the story of Jacob's life after he left his parents. (Jacob was Sarah and Abraham's grandson.) Jacob had a dream of angels ascending a ladder from earth to heaven, and descending from heaven back down to earth. God appeared in the dream and gave Jacob a promise that was very similar to the promise God had given Sarah and Abraham many years before. (Remember Genesis 12—building your altar?)

Throughout the Bible, angels are messengers of God. They tell us things, they protect, they serve God, they honor and worship God and Christ. Remember the angels, remember the promises of God today as you try an experiment. Think of the ladder that the angels in Jacob's dream climbed up and then down. Then, take some time to climb a literal flight of stairs.

On each step, stop. Ask the Spirit of God who or what you should pray for. Pray for that person. Ask again, pray again on the next step. Don't be surprised if the Spirit gently leads you to pray for people or groups of people you don't even know, or for situations you don't know much about. Be open. What do you notice? Is there any prayer you're supposed to continue praying in the days to come?

Notes, drawings, thoughts:

Prayer: If you know it, sing the song "We are climbing Jacob's ladder / We are climbing Jacob's ladder / We are climbing Jacob's ladder / Soldiers of the Cross [*or* Brothers, Sisters all]."

"Every round goes higher, higher..."

"Sinners do you love your Jesus?..."

"If you love him, why not serve him?..."

"We are climbing Jacob's ladder..."

If you don't know the song, pray the words, then ask someone who went to church camp to teach you the tune!

Searching Cracks in the Floor for a Quarter

Scripture: Luke 15:1–10

If you have time today, read all of chapter 15 in the gospel of Luke. It's incredible. Here are three stories of the lost: a lost sheep, a lost coin, a lost son. And in each story the searcher (shepherd, woman, father) goes to unbelievable lengths to get back what is missing. The shepherd leaves 99 sheep in the wilderness to get back one stray. The woman rearranges furniture, sweeps, practically tears up floorboards to get back the coin. And you probably know what the father does.

Pray. Pray now. Ask God to show you people who are lost, who are far from home, who are floundering, no matter how good their circumstances look on the surface. Ask Jesus to let you see them with his eyes, to yearn for them with his heart. Ask the Spirit to let your heart break for them if it needs to.

Then pray for them. And do anything for them you're supposed to do.

Notes, drawings, thoughts:

Prayer: Lord, help me to care. Open my eyes. Unlock my heart. Direct my steps toward whomever you need me to love, to care for. I want to help others because I love you. Amen.

Reflection Day

REVIEW. Think back over your week of prayer. Reread your favorite scripture from the week. Review your notes, lists, insights. How is your prayer going? Review the introduction to Part Three, beginning on page 115. Which ideas from the introduction do you need to pay attention to this week? Take some notes.

Then, answer two questions:

Question 1: What are the most important things I've learned/discovered/remembered this week?

Question 2: God, what one insight would you like me to share with my study group when we meet?

Prayer:

I asked for strength that I might achieve;
I was made weak that I might learn humbly to obey.
I asked for health that I might do greater things;
I was given infirmity that I might do better things.
I asked for riches that I might be happy;
I was given poverty that I might be wise.
I asked for power that I might have the praise of men;
I was given weakness that I might feel the need of God.
I asked for all things that I might enjoy life;
I was given life that I might enjoy all things.
I got nothing that I had asked for,
but everything that I had hoped for.
Almost despite myself my unspoken prayers were answered;
I am, among all men, most richly blessed.

Unknown soldier, 19th century, American Civil War

Group Meeting Day

Enjoy your time to talk, laugh and pray together! Tell each other what you've learned. Pray together.

Notes & insights:

Prayer:

Lord, you are to be blessed and praised;
all good things come from you:
you are in our words and in our thoughts,
and in all that we do. Amen.

St. Teresa of Avila, 16th century, Spain

Praying with Scripture

Scripture: Psalm 139:1–12

Breathe in and out slowly. Inhale the peace of Christ; exhale any worries or tensions you are dragging around. Breathe in and out slowly until you are ready to listen. Be still for a minute or so and let God be with you in the silence. When you are ready, read the scripture.

Do you remember this psalm from our first day of prayer? You may be a little different than three weeks ago. Will you read the psalm again slowly and see if God speaks to you through it again? Which lines seem most important? Sit quietly for several minutes. Be aware of how God is present with you.

Now read the psalm again, slowly. Rest in the silence. What words feel most "emphasized," or shine out at you?

Read the psalm portion one more time, and stay in the silence. Is God showing you different things today (about the psalm, or about yourself) than three Mondays ago?

Notes, drawings, thoughts:

Prayer: Thank you, God. Thank you that I cannot escape you, no matter how hard I try. Amen.

Remember Your Baptism

Scripture: Matthew 3

John the Baptist told the Jews (read "people who have been in church all their lives") not to presume their lives are fine because they were on the cradle roll at church! We, too, must repent and hand our lives over to God. Jesus was baptized by John. A voice from heaven proclaimed, "This is my Son, the Beloved, with whom I am well pleased." St. Paul said that we are baptized into Jesus' baptism and so shall be raised with him from death into the glorious resurrection.

Martin Luther, who suffered from horrible depressions, had one consolation during his darkest moments. "I remember my baptism." We're thinking about new members, new Christians in *Unbinding Your Heart*. How can we remember our baptisms and what they mean?

Sit and think in the silence for a few minutes. Ask God to show you what still frightens you. What worries you? What sins have accumulated since your baptism?

Stand now and go to the sink. Turn on the water. Listen to it flowing freely. Take a deep breath in and think of all that frightens, worries and makes you feel guilty or regret-filled. Ask for forgiveness. Hand each of those things to God, one by one. Feel each burden leaving your body, through your hands, into the water. Let the water carry them away. Say, "I remember my baptism. Thank you, God."

Each time you wash your hands this week, breathe in, breathe out, remember that you are pardoned, freed, adopted as God's child. Let the old go into the water. Remember your baptism.

Notes, drawings, thoughts:

Prayer: God, thank you for forgiving me, for making me a new creation. Thank you that I am yours—pardoned, saved and in Christ's body, the church. Amen.

Peace and Safety

Scripture: Philippians 4:4–7; Isaiah 43:1–7

What are you afraid of? Make a list. We live in a scary world. We live with illnesses, gimpy knees, fragile hearts, failing pension plans, terrorism, wars and fears of all sorts of things. We worry about children, jobs, futures, families, money, friends. Christians worry, and you can be sure that people who do **not** have a conscious relationship with God or a loving church home are afraid, too.

Our God is the God of peace. Read these passages (remember the "rejoice always" words from Paul? We've read them before!). Sink into the peace of Isaiah's prophesy. Read and reread these passages. Say the words aloud. FEEL the safety of God pulsing through your body with the beating of your heart. Sit quietly for a few minutes, experiencing the peace, the security of God.

Now place your hands loosely in your lap, palms up, little fingers touching. Imagine someone who is afraid, "shrunk to small size" and in your hands. Let the peace of God, which passes understanding, surround and permeate the person you are holding in prayer. Ask God who else you are to pray for this way, especially people who don't know Christ, or who have no church community. God may ask you to pray for people who are total strangers.

Notes, drawings, thoughts:

Prayer:

I arise today, Christ with me, Christ before me, Christ behind me,
Christ in me, Christ beneath me, Christ above me,
Christ on my right, Christ on my left,
Christ when I lie down, Christ when I sit down, Christ when I arise,
Christ in the heart of everyone who thinks of me,
Christ in the mouth of everyone who speaks of me,
Christ in every eye that sees me, Christ in every ear that hears me.
I arise today through a mighty strength, the invocation of the Trinity,
Through belief in the threeness, through confession of the oneness,
Of the Creator of Creation.

St. Patrick's Breastplate (Part of a Celtic prayer from the 7th or 8th century, Ireland)

Faith in the World

Scripture: Philippians 1:12–14

Paul writes to the church at Philippi from a Roman prison. With Paul, jail is just as good a place as any to come into contact with people who do not know the good news of Jesus Christ. Some of you reading this today may be in jail yourselves. Please know that our prayers are with you and that your ministry to those around you matters to the whole church. Thank you.

Today is a field-trip prayer day. You may want to use your lunch hour at work. Before you go, pray with this scripture and ask the Spirit where you should go. Choose a place—a coffee shop, a cafeteria, a train station—any place people will be sitting and talking. First ask God if it's okay for you to be aware of what the people around you are saying. If you have any doubt, move to a different seat. If you sense that it's all right with God to be aware of conversations around you, sit quietly, listen to people and pray for them.

What are these people's lives like? Pray for them, quietly, from your corner, as the Spirit moves you. Do you have any inclination to smile at someone, to say something? Pay attention to the Spirit's promptings. Can you obey them?

Notes, drawings, thoughts:

Prayer: Beloved Jesus, please ask your Spirit to lead me through this watching and listening time. Show me your people through *your* eyes. Let me pray *your* prayers for them. Amen.

The Jesus Prayer—Praying without Ceasing

Supplies: a string of pearls, beads, Mardi Gras beads, prayer beads—anything to hold in your hands, to pass from one hand to another. Or be ready to walk. Or to sit and breathe!

Scripture: 1 Thessalonians 5:16–22

What did Paul mean when he said to "pray without ceasing"? Many Eastern Orthodox monks believe that if we pray simply and often enough, we begin to pray all the time. Our hearts beat in time with the prayer, our breath is synchronized with it. Their prayer is very simple: Lord Jesus Christ, Son of God, have mercy on me, a sinner.

Some people pray the prayer without the last phrase, "a sinner." You choose, or experiment with both. You can pray this prayer many, many ways. I love to pray holding a string of some kind of beads. Hold the first bead and think "Lord Jesus Christ" and inhale very slowly. As you exhale slowly, think "Son of God." Inhale with "have mercy on me," and exhale with "a sinner." Shift that bead into your right hand (or left, if you are left-handed) and pray the same way on the second bead.

You can pray without the beads, just using your breath to feel the rhythm of the prayer. You can whisper the words. You can walk and take a step for each of the four "steps" of the prayer. Pray the Jesus prayer for a long time. When you are finished, thank God.

Notes, drawings, thoughts:

Prayer: Lord Jesus Christ, Son of God, have mercy on me, a sinner. Please help me pray without ceasing. Amen.

Reflection Day

REVIEW. Think back over your week of prayer. Reread your favorite scripture from the week. Review your notes, lists, insights. How is your prayer going? Review the introduction to Part Three, beginning on page 115. Which ideas from the introduction do you need to pay attention to this week? Take some notes.

Then, answer two questions:

Question 1: What are the most important things I've learned/discovered/remembered this week?

Question 2: God, what one insight would you like me to share with my study group when we meet?

Prayer: Almighty God, and most merciful Father, who didst command the Children of Israel to offer a daily Sacrifice to Thee, that thereby they might Glorify and Praise Thee for Thy Protection both Night and Day, Receive, O Lord, my Morning Sacrifice which I now Offer up to Thee; I yield Thee humble and hearty Thanks that Thou has Preserved me from the Danger of the Night Past, and Brought me to the Light of the Day, and the Comforts thereof, a Day which is Consecrated to Thine own Service and for Thine own Honor.

George Washington, 18th century, United States

Group Meeting Day

Enjoy your time to talk, laugh and pray together! Tell each other what you've learned. Pray together.

Notes & insights:

Prayer: O God, please help me to be sensitive to all the people you could use me to show your love and to tell about you. If I'm being oblivious, please get my attention! Amen.

God's Love in Christ

Scripture: Romans 8:35–39

Do you remember praying with this passage from Monday of our second week?

Sit quietly for a minute, breathing slowly, letting go of thoughts and feelings. Just be with God. As you exhale, feel as if you are living in the very center of your body, where you breathe.

Now read St. Paul's words slowly. Which lines speak to you most powerfully?

Sit in the silence with God for several more minutes. Now read the scripture again, slowly. What words shine out at you? Offer God several more minutes of silence. Just be with God. What do you notice? Is God showing you different things than three weeks ago?

Notes, drawings, thoughts:

Prayer: Lord Jesus, thank you. Thank you that nothing can separate me from you. Amen.

Jesus Gives Us All Power; Pack Nothing for the Trip

Scripture: John 14:12–14; Luke 9:1–6

Jesus says that after his death and resurrection we will be able to do miracles even greater than his. We will be able to do greater miracles **because God will send us the Holy Spirit** (John 14). In the passage from St. Luke, Jesus sent out the twelve disciples. He gave them power and authority over all demons and to cure diseases. He gave them authority to proclaim the kingdom of God and to heal. Then he told them to take no luggage. Just one outfit. Just themselves. Just **go**.

Jesus offers **us** lives of tremendous spiritual power and authority. Jesus will use us if we are willing to leave our baggage at home and get out the door.

Will you sit for a few minutes in the silence with Christ and ask what is keeping you from accepting his offer of a life of spiritual power? What old baggage are you clutching to your bosom? What barriers are you using to fence Christ out, to keep him backed off to a "safe" distance?

Look at Christ. What does he say? Is he asking you to hand those extra pounds you're carrying to him?

Notes, drawings, thoughts:

Prayer: Lord Jesus, thank you for helping me to see what I'm using to block your power in my life. Please help me hand it to you. Now, please use me as much as you can trust me. Please use me to do your miraculous work. Please do miracles through our church. Amen.

See; Remember

Scripture: Psalm 136

Psalm 136 is a remembering psalm. Israel remembers and gives thanks to God for all God's steadfast love, for all God's great and mighty works toward the people Israel. Jews and Christians have remembered for 4,000 years—the Passover, the Exodus, the Exile, the Return to Jerusalem. God can open our eyes and enrich our lives when we see what God has done, when we remember, when we tell the stories.

What has God done in your life over these last five weeks? What have you seen? Learned? Heard? Recognized? Let go of? What has God shown you?

Go back through this journal, through your notes in this book. Think. Ask God in the silence. Then write here what you do not want to forget. Hear, O Israel, and remember; for his steadfast love endures forever.

Notes, drawings, thoughts:

Prayer: Holy One of Israel, over the coming days, help me to see more, understand more of what you want to teach me. Help me to remember what you show. Thank you. Amen.

What about the New Ones?

Scripture: Galatians 6:11–16

The biggest disagreement in the early church was about how "Jewish" the new converts had to be. Did they need to be circumcised? Did they have to follow the entire Jewish law? Paul said no. James insisted upon full compliance. Peter waffled. He said different things, depending on to whom he was talking. (Read the middle of Galatians chapter 2 to see how impressed Paul was with *that!*) They all finally came to an agreement. The new Gentile converts only had to obey the pared-down essentials of the law so that they would get the main point. (See vv. 14–15).

We have a similar predicament today. It's not about circumcision or what to eat. We're more likely to wonder about ways we do worship or Christian education, or how "churchily" we name and decorate things. One of the key questions over the ages has been "How do we figure out which parts of the faith we've grown up with are *faith essentials*, as opposed to *ways* we've helped specific generations *understand* *the essentials*?" Missionaries have always had to make these evaluations. St. Patrick was the son of a fairly wealthy Roman family living in Britain. When he went to Ireland, first as a kidnapped slave, then as a missionary, he did what Paul did with the Gentiles. Patrick preached the love and forgiveness of God through Jesus Christ as the heart of the faith. He expressed these eternals in the way the Irish could see and hear them, using "indigenous" Celtic art, language and culture.

Sit quietly. Breathe slowly. Ask God to show you a few things that are the very core of the faith, the essence of Christianity. Then think about some of the unchurched people you know. Could they get snagged or stopped in their journey toward Christ by little ways we've always done things? How can we help them see what really matters—that Christ loves and forgives them? that the church is a power-filled community that loves and serves the world? Ask Christ to show you a few specific things your church could do to help new people fit in and understand the faith more easily.

Notes, drawings, thoughts:

Prayer: God, help me to keep first things first! Help me to remember that the point of our faith is your love for us, your forgiveness, that power of life as a member of the body of Christ, to begin a life of essentials, of eternals! Help us be sensitive to new people's reactions and needs. Let me remember to ASK them, not assume! Amen.

Light of the World

Scripture: Matthew 5:14–16

This passage is from the Sermon on the Mount. Jesus tells the crowds of people that they are the salt of the earth, the light of the world. Jesus wants us to let our light shine for others. *You* are the light of the world. Put your light on a lampstand. Shine in public. Let people see your faith, your good works.

Pray slowly with this passage. Sit in silence. Read it again. Listen to what the Spirit may be showing you about how it applies in your life and your ministry.

Now, with closed eyes, imagine that the Spirit is inside you, at the center of your body or in your heart. Feel the Spirit as light. Feel it shining through your body. Imagine the Spirit healing anything that needs healing in you, then shining even more brightly. Feel your face shining with the light of Christ. See the light radiating out of your whole self, toward others. Know that the light of Christ, the knowledge of Christ, the power of Christ's Spirit is in you.

Ask God to let others see Christ's light in you, to feel Christ's love and power in you. Remember. You are the light of the world. Shine so that people who don't know Jesus can see his face. Keep alert as you live today for a person who may need to see Christ's light in you.

Notes, drawings, thoughts:

Prayer: Oh Spirit of God, please shine in me. Heal me. Help me to hand you anything in my life—sin, opinions, preconceptions, possessions—that keeps me from being available to you. You may use me to be Jesus' love and light to the people I meet today. Amen.

Reflection Day

REVIEW. Think back over your week of prayer. Reread your favorite scripture from the week. Review your notes, lists, insights. How is your prayer going? Review the introduction to Part Three, beginning on page 115. Which ideas from the introduction do you need to pay attention to this week? Take some notes.

Then, answer two questions:

Question 1: What are the most important things I've learned/discovered/remembered this week?

Question 2: God, what one insight would you like me to share with my study group when we meet?

Prayer:

Lord, make me an instrument of your peace.
Where there is hatred, let me sow love,
Where there is injury, pardon,
Where there is doubt, faith,
Where there is despair, hope,
Where there is darkness, light,
Where there is sadness, joy.
O Divine Master, grant that I may not so much
seek to be consoled as to console,
not so much to be understood as to understand,
not so much to be loved, as to love;
for it is in giving that we receive,
it is in pardoning that we are pardoned,
it is in dying that we awake to eternal life.

St. Francis of Assisi, 13th century, Italy

Group Meeting Day

Enjoy your time to talk, laugh and pray together! Tell each other what you've learned. Pray together.

Notes & insights:

Prayer: O Lord our God, under the shadow of Thy wings let us hope. Thou wilt support us, both when little and even to gray hairs. When our strength is of Thee, it is strength; but, when our own, it is feebleness. We return unto Thee, O Lord, that from their weariness our souls may rise towards Thee, leaning on the thing which Thou has created, and passing on to Thyself, who hast wonderfully made them; for with Thee is refreshment and true strength. Amen.

St. Augustine of Hippo, 4th century, Africa (present-day Algeria)

Another Hour with the Spirit

Scripture: John 14:16–26

As Jesus prepared his disciples for his leaving, he told them he would be gone *and* with them. God would send the Spirit. The Holy Spirit is available to us today, as Christ's disciples. The Spirit will give us guidance, power, minute-by-minute connection with God. Have you felt the Spirit more vividly at some point during the last five weeks?

Will you try an experiment again? Ask God to show you the Spirit—give God another hour this week, as you did three weeks ago. Pick your hour, but a different one than before. It may be an exercise hour. Ask whether to bike, run or walk. Ask the Spirit to show you where to turn. If it's a shopping hour, turn every decision over. Hamburger, chicken or portabello mushrooms? Which aisle should you go down next? Should you say something to that lady over there? Smile at the boy stocking shelves? Let the Spirit pilot you all over the store. Just remember—at every choice point during the hour, ask the Spirit what you're supposed to do. Ask!

What happened?

Notes, drawings, thoughts:

Prayer: Come, Holy Spirit! Please show me how you can be with me every day, every minute. Please come into my life, be with me, help me toward holiness, direct my thoughts and steps. Make me completely yours. Amen.

Serenity

Scripture: Psalm 127:1–2; Proverbs 3:5–6

Be open to the words of these scriptures. Unless God is in our work, it won't matter much in the long run. We must trust in God, not our own insight. Read this psalm and the proverb slowly. Think about them. What do they say to you? How do they speak into your life?

Do you know anyone who has spent years in a 12-step program (Alcoholics Anonymous, Al-Anon, Overeaters Anonymous, etc.)? Recovering alcoholics can be tremendously authentic. They often learn crucial lessons about letting God set the pace and not "pushing the river." They pray the Serenity Prayer. They learn layers of the prayer's meaning over years. If you know someone like this, will you invite that person out for coffee and ask about waiting on God's timing? Ask about trust. Ask about serenity.

Notes, drawings, thoughts:

Prayer: God grant me the serenity to accept the things I cannot change; courage to change the things I can; and wisdom to know the difference.

Alcoholic Anonymous' Serenity Prayer, based on a prayer by Reinhold Niebuhr, 20th century, United States

Peace

Scripture: Psalm 122:6–9; John 14:25–27

We have all experienced "non-peace." All friendships stumble occasionally. Every family has times of coolness (or way too much heat!) Workplace relationships can twist your stomach into knots. Too many of us know the feel of church conflict. We live in a world of wars and rumors of wars. Yet Christ left us his Spirit and his peace. The psalm tells us to pray for peace for the sake of the people, for the sake of the city and the house of God. ***How*** do we pray for peace?

Remember how you have prayed for individuals? Try this as a prayer for peace. First, sit quietly in the silence. Meditate on one of the scriptures that draws your attention. Ask God to gentle your spirit and thoughts so that you can be a vessel for Christ's peace. When you are more still, more peaceful yourself, hold your hands, palms up, in your lap. Ask God to place in your hands whatever or whomever you should pray for. Ask the Spirit to immerse you and those for whom you pray in God's peace. The people or situations in your hands may shift to others. Continue for as long as you sense the Spirit wants you to pray.

Notes, drawings, thoughts:

Prayer:

Lamb of God, who takes away the sins of the world, have mercy on us.
Lamb of God, who takes away the sins of the world, have mercy on us.
Lamb of God, who takes away the sins of the world, grant us peace.

Ancient Latin Prayer, the Agnus Dei ("Lamb of God")

Walk to Emmaus—Jesus' Last Words according to Luke

Scripture: Luke 24:13–52

Hope Tinsley Benko, a wonderful, young Episcopal priest, says that if she could only have one bit of scripture, this would be enough. God could use it to teach her the rest! In a way, everything *is* here. Here's the power and might of God revealed in Christ's death and resurrection. Here, on the road to Emmaus, Jesus shows the disciples a great truth that's hidden to them. He teaches them patiently, kindly, as he always taught. Now he offers to teach us. Here is the first communion—not Jesus telling about the Lord's Supper, as he did in the upper room the night before he died—but in one way the *real* first communion, where the disciples recognize that the man they've been talking to all afternoon is the risen Lord. They see him for who he is as they eat together.

Read the Walk to Emmaus story slowly. Be still. Read it again. Be still. Read it again and, in the silence, see the hidden thing the Lord has to show you.

Notes, drawings, thoughts:

Prayer: Risen Jesus, risen Lord, thank you for your power and majesty. Thank you for your Spirit in my life. Let me be your true disciple. Please, show me what I haven't seen. Let me hear sounds to which I've been deaf. Help me slow down. Help me understand people and situations with your wisdom. Amen.

To the End of the Age—Jesus' Last Words according to Matthew

Scripture: Matthew 28:16–20

This is the "Great Commission." It's the Bible passage we Christians often use to flog ourselves into enough guilt to pry some evangelism out of us! How have we let this glorious promise, trust, and challenge become the blunt instrument of "Oughts" and "Shoulds"?

If we hear the promise of Christ's presence with us forever, into eternity, how can we shrink from these words? We are entrusted with the precious people Jesus leaves as he goes to the Father in heaven. These dear ones are left in our care—confused, not knowing, lonely, afraid, some young, some old, some wealthy, some scrambling for rent money—all made for God and not knowing it yet.

Pray with this passage. Sit with Jesus in silence. Ask him what he wants to tell you. Ask him if there is anything he'll let you do for him.

Notes, drawings, thoughts:

Prayer: Lord Jesus, Precious One. Thank you. Thank you that you will be with us forever, until you bring us into your unadulterated, shining presence. Use me. Use what is left of my life. Help me see that these aren't your last words to me, but some of your first! I love you. Amen.

Reflection Day

REVIEW. Think back over your week of prayer. Reread your favorite scripture from the week. Review your notes, lists, insights. How is your prayer going? Review the introduction to Part Three, beginning on page 115. Which ideas from the introduction do you need to pay attention to this week? Take some notes.

Then, answer two questions:

Question 1: What are the most important things I've learned/discovered/remembered this week?

Question 2: God, what one insight would you like me to share with my study group when we meet?

Afterword

I went to my doctor this morning. It was a routine checkup. I need to see him every quarter to make sure that the medications that are supposed to help my blood pressure and cholesterol aren't damaging my liver. Our visits are usually very brief—you know, blood test results, blood pressure, temperature, pulse, followed by, "How are you feeling? Any problems?" to which I answer, "I feel fantastic. No worries at all," and he tells me to come back in three months.

But today was different. My doctor knows that I am a Christian, because it came up in an earlier conversation, maybe a year ago. So today he comes in and says, right off the bat, "I have a question for you. You know, I'm getting older, and that makes any sane person think about their mortality, their spirit… You know what I mean. But any time I begin to feel closer to God, I hear some wacko on TV say something absolutely outrageous in the name of God or religion, and it just smothers my interest. It pushes me in the totally opposite direction."

He said he had a question, but it was left unexpressed. It didn't matter, because with or without a specific question to get us started, we ended up having a good conversation. Three things are still kind of vibrating inside of me from that conversation.

First, people like my doctor—intelligent people, thoughtful, honest people—really want to talk about God and the spiritual life. In spite of the important statistics Martha Grace Reese presents, in spite of the fact that, generation by generation, fewer Americans identify themselves as religious, everywhere I go I find people like my doctor who are thinking about life, its meaning, its destiny, their souls, their purpose, God. And they want to talk. They need to talk. And they need a conversation partner.

Second, there are plenty of religious wackos around who talk about God a lot. Whatever the religion, there are people who abuse it and say "absolutely outrageous" things "in the name of God or religion," as my doctor said.

And third, there are plenty of sincere and generous people of faith around, too, who would be great conversation partners for people like my doctor. But here's the problem: so many of them are so afraid of sounding like the wackos that they keep their faith to themselves.

Their silence, of course, makes the strident and outrageous voices seem all the louder, and so their silence ends up being complicit in smothering the interest of the spiritual seekers.

That's why Martha Grace Reese's book is so important. That's why when you turn the last page, you can't let this be just another book you read. You need to let her message affect you, and your faith community, and, through you, people like my doctor.

Her image of the pitcher being filled to overflowing is worth the price of the book. Her insight that there can be many sources of motivation and inspiration for faith sharing—many ways to fill the pitcher to the brim—rings very true to me. The statistics she gives sober me, and they motivate me too. And her stories of vibrant congregations give me hope.

Especially today, after my conversation with my doctor.

On my way home from the doctor's office, I turned on the radio and caught the news. More violence. More bad news about global warming. More political division and rancorous

161

name-calling. More stories of people abusing people sexually, kids with guns, crooked politicians, corrupt business executives.

I thought to myself, "What can change this vicious cycle of viciousness?" I switched the radio off as I drove along in silence. I remembered the famous quote from the 19th-century British statesman, Edmund Burke: "All that the forces of evil need to win in this world is for enough good people to do nothing," or something to that effect.

I thought, "Somebody should start an organization that would mobilize people—recruit them, train them, support them—so they could be good people who do something so that the forces of evil don't win in this world. This organization would need to accept people just as they are, infuse them with hope, give them a vision of a better world, give them a vision for themselves becoming agents of making that better world a reality. It would need to both practice and preach. Why hasn't somebody started an organization like that?"

And, of course, about a quarter mile down the road I realized that somebody had done just that. In fact, it had cost him everything to do so.

But that organization can become so preoccupied with lesser things—including its own institutional survival—that it forgets why it's really here: to recruit people to switch sides and opt out of the vicious cycle and join a cycle of healing, to infuse them with vision, to send them out as change agents, to help them experience transformation and sustain them so they can be lifelong catalysts of transformation, to give them good news to share to counter the bad news that is being reported every hour on the hour.

When you close the covers of Martha Grace Reese's book, I wonder if you could say a prayer asking God to empower you to help your faith community become the kind of organization that Jesus intended it to be, the kind of organization that helps people like my doctor, the kind of organization that brings good news in a bad-news world.

And if your faith community is hopelessly stuck in the mud—let's face it, some are—then don't let that get you down. You have a kitchen table, right? Then invite some friends over and get them talking. Ask them about their faith stories. Ask them about their beliefs about God. Ask them about what kind of world they see, and what kind they dream of, and what they're doing about it, and how God might fit in. Make it clear there aren't "right answers"—just honest answers—and see what happens. See what God does around your table.

If you don't have a kitchen table, invite a friend out for coffee, or take a walk. Don't preach. Just do what Martha Grace talks about in this book. And pray that God will somehow use you to be a blessing to somebody by being an available conversation partner about the things that matter most in life.

You don't need anyone's permission to do this. You don't need a committee or a budget. You don't need a degree in theology or (God forbid) sales and marketing. You just need a pitcher full of motivation—and Martha Grace has given that to you in this book. Let it overflow. Let it pour.

Brian McLaren (brianmclaren.net)

Works Cited

Here is a short list of the books referred to in this work. See **www.GraceNet.info** for more information: a bibliography of books, Web sites, sociological studies; a congregational hospitality survey; a full sociological report on the Mainline Evangelism Study's survey of congregations that are doing the best job reaching unchurched people, and other resources that may be helpful to you.

Collins, Jim. *Built to Last: Successful Habits of Visionary Companies*. New York: HarperBusiness Essentials, 2002.

Craddock, Fred. *Craddock Stories*. Edited by Mike Graves and Richard F. Ward. St. Louis: Chalice Press, 2001.

Dillard, Annie. *Teaching a Stone to Talk*. Toronto: HarperCollins Publishers, 1988.

Driskill, Joseph D. *Protestant Spiritual Exercises: Theology, History, and Practice*. Harrisburg, Pa.: Morehouse Publishing, 1999.

Duke University. *Survey of Clergy*. www.pulpitandpew.duke.edu/research.html.

Foster, Richard J. *Prayer: Finding the Heart's True Home*. New York: HarperCollins Publishers, 1992.

Haugk, Kenneth C. *Antagonists in the Church: How to Identify and Deal with Destructive Conflict*. Minneapolis: Augsburg Publishing House, 1988.

Hunter, George G., III. *The Celtic Way of Evangelism: How Christianity Can Reach the West.... Again*. Nashville: Abingdon Press, 2000.

____. *Church for the Unchurched*. Nashville: Abingdon Press, 1996.

McLaren, Brian D. *A New Kind of Christian: A Tale of Two Christians on a Spiritual Journey*. San Francisco: Jossey-Bass, 2001.

Marshall, Peter. *The Best of Peter Marshall*. Compiled and edited by Catherine Marshall. Old Tappan, N.J.: Fleming H. Revell Co., 1983.

Montgomery, Lucy M. *Anne's House of Dreams*. New York: Grossett and Dunlap, 1917.

Osmer, Richard Robert. *A Teachable Spirit*. Louisville: Westminster/John Knox Press, 1990.

Payne, Claude, and Hamilton Beazley. *Reclaiming the Great Commission: A Practical Model for Transforming Denominations and Congregations*. New York: Jossey-Bass, 2000.

Peterson, Eugene. *The Message*. Colorado Springs: NavPress, 1995.

Schwartz, Christian. *Natural Church Development: A Guide to Eight Essential Qualities of Healthy Churches*. Carol Stream, Ill.: Church Smart Resources, 1996.

Smith, Tom W. "The Vanishing Protestant Majority." *GSS Social Change Report No. 49*. Chicago: NORC/University of Chicago, July 2004. (http://www.norc.uchicago.edu/issues/PROTSG08.pdf).

Tuchman, Barbara. *Practicing History*. New York: Alfred A. Knopf, 1981.

**For Best Results
download free "Best Practices" memo
at *www.GraceNet.info*
Before You Start**

Before you start the Unbinding Series in your church, download the latest updates of our organizational resources. Our 10 years of Lilly Endowment-funded research with 3000 congregations reveals startling findings on the best ways to get started. Maximize your results! Use our easy-to-follow, step-by-step, Best Practices Guide for the most powerful impact.

Also download free Unbinding supplementary resources (embedded in the Best Practices Guide at www.GraceNet.info). Find resources for children and youth, coordinated sermons, music and worship plans, organizational planning guides and checklists, retreat plans, prayer resources, promotional materials and detailed research results.